THE
ELECTORAL
COLLEGE
and the
BLACK
and
BROWN
VOTE

THE
ELECTORAL
COLLEGE
and the
BLACK
and
BROWN
VOTE

—Versus—
The National Popular Vote Interstate Compact,
Popular Plurality, and One Person, One Vote

VAL ATKINSON

To order additional copies of this book, contact:
Xlibris
844-714-8691
www.Xlibris.com
Orders@Xlibris.com
828211

Val Atkinson — *Author*

Courtesy, "Val Atkinson Photos"

Is the Electoral College a viable process for electing a president to serve a multi-racial, multi-ethnic electorate?

HAS ITS TIME PASSED? ARE AMERICANS CAPABLE OF CHOOSING THEIR LEADERS BY POPULAR VOTE, UNASSISTED BY AN ARCHAIC 18th CENTURY ELECTORAL SYSTEM? ARE AMERICANS STILL AFRAID OF SECESSION?

CONTENTS

DEDICATION

*T*his book it dedicated to Johnson Lassiter Atkinson Jr., our 4th grandchild, and the cutest of them all by far... **and this has been progressively the case since Victor Lorenzo Atkinson, and Graham & Ellis St. Cyr.**

Val Atkinson
with Grandson, JJ (Johnson Lassiter Atkinson Jr.)

Courtesy "Val Atkinson Photos"

I also dedicate this with special love for my late grandson Victor Lorenzo Atkinson. Victor passed away unexpectantly year before last. He was just 26 years old. Rest In Peace Victor.

ACKNOWLEDGEMENTS

The completion of this book would have been more difficult had the following people not shared their knowledge, skills, and counsel with me as I ventured down this literary path: Dr. Artemesia Stanberry, Dr. Donnell Scott, Rev. Dr. George Herman Spicer, Vincent "Ed" Clark, Dwight "DC" Collins, Cornelius "Jack" Herbert, Connie Walton, Richard "Pedro" Smith, Richard "Rip" Turner, Vincent "Sonny" Hargraves, Barbara West Davis, Harold Valentinus Atkinson Jr., Cheryll Elizabeth Atkinson, J'né Dorothea Atkinson St. Cyr, her husband Bernell "Saint" St. Cyr, Michelle Cox – Atkinson and her husband Johnson Lassiter Atkinson Sr. ... and to my lovely wife of 38 years — *Juju.*

I want to give a special acknowledgement to those involved in our Random Survey: Michael and Debbie Okoli, Scott and Jean Kobida, Bernell & Patrice St. Cyr, Maurice and Earlene Hardie -Cox, Andre and Colette Paxton-Gingles, Sally Sims-Murrell, Constance Lowe, Carol Parker, Brenda Ann Atkinson-Young, Hilda Atkinson-Holt, Carrie Mae Atkinson, Vernon Hodges, Ray Jackson, Ethlene "Janet" Jackson-Harris, Iris Tucker, Jackie Avery, Gina Mack, Cynthia Gongs, James Grier, Jackie Upperman, David Pickett, Jennifer Hodges, Mary Best and Luby Best Jr.

Atkinsons, Beverlys, Tolberts, Gingles and St. Cyrs Family Photo

Courtesy "Val Atkinson Photos"

FOREWORD

By Vincent "Ed" Clark

"There could be no greater example of why the framers felt that the Congress needed impeachment powers to control an out-of-control chief executive officer than the antics of Donald Trump."

"There could be no greater example of why we need the 25th Amendment than the encompassing incompetency of Donald Trump."

"There could be no greater example of why the framers allowed Faithless Electors in the Electoral College than the 2016 Electoral College election of Donald Trump."

Val & Ed at Foxy 107-104 Radio Station

Courtesy, "Val Atkinson Photos"

In this book Val lays bare the struggles the framers had with *Article II* as they carefully and cautiously approached the daunting task of determining how the president of the United States would be selected.

He methodically discusses the pros and cons of alternatives to the Electoral College, and he offers his personal choice with supporting rationalizations. Finally, he examines the impact that the Electoral College has on the presumption of *"One Person – One Vote"*, with particular emphasis on its impact on the vote of minorities *(The Black and Brown Vote)*. The impact that the Electoral College has on the minority vote is (in my opinion) the most striking and therefore deserves to be mentioned in the books title ... **"The Electoral College and _The Black and Brown Vote_"**. The publication timing was spot-on. The presidential election of 2020 will go down as the 2nd most directional election in the history of the United States of America.

I believe that factions within the conservative movement in America came to the conclusion (after the 2012 re-election of President Barack Obama and the demographic projections for 2042) that winning elections going forward within the current electoral framework would be very, very difficult if not impossible. They therefore went about the business of changing, bending and ignoring the rules. There were three elements of electoral politics that didn't bode well for conservatives: *(1) Campaign Finance Laws and Regulations (2)The Preclearance Requirements of the 1965 Voting Rights Act (3) and Fair Redistricting (a lack of Gerrymandering)*. The campaign finance road block was largely resolved when the court ruled on *"Citizens United"*. This ruling allows *dark money* to control American politics as it has never done before. Citizens United literally allowed donors to *buy* politicians, and thereby buy elections. When Chief Justice John Roberts sided with the four conservative justices on the Supreme Court and ruled that Section 4 of the 1965 Voting Rights Act was unconstitutional, it was tantamount to ruling that the entire Voting Rights Act was unconstitutional. Section 4 identifies those states, or portions thereof, that should come under the auspices of the Act. Without Section 4 the Act is toothless. It has no basis to hold any state or section thereof accountable under the primary provisions of the Act (Section 5, or Preclearance). And without Preclearance requirements, some states (Pennsylvania, Texas and North Carolina) couldn't wait to change voting laws and regulations to hamper the voting powers of minority voters, young voters, and members of any group that consistently voted for Democratic candidates.

Gerrymandering became an issue when states such as North Carolina used *run-away* Gerrymandering to change their Congressional Delegation from a 7-6 Democrat majority to a 10-3 Republican majority. All this occurred with the state's registered voters being almost evenly divided between Democrat, Unaffiliate and Republican voters (40%, 30% and 30% respectively). The supreme court ruling in *"Rucho v Common Cause"* (another North Carolina case) gave Republican legislative majorities another boost when it decided that it *was* constitutional for state legislatures to practice hyper-partisanship when carrying out the redistricting process.

With these three measures in place it may become difficult to recognize America as a *"One Person, One Vote Democracy"*. With the aforementioned issues running in the background, it's easy to see why a growing number of Americans and foreigners wonder if we're headed in the right electoral direction. The need for some Americans to maintain their perceived culture is so great that they don't believe that any custom, practice, or law should stand in the way of their access to what some have labeled AWMCC, or *"American White Male Christian Culture"*. We are well aware that before the election of Barack Obama as the 44th President of the United States of America, only white males had occupied the office of President of the United States. The first Obama election in 2008 was seen as an aberration by some conservatives, but the reelection of President Obama in 2012 was too much for many of them to take. And then, after two terms of Barack Obama the Democratic Party nominated a female to become the 45th President of the United States. **That was it!** *The horse had left the barn, the chickens had flown the coop, and the shoe was on the other foot.* Any and everything was on the table now. Republicans didn't need a curator to audit the inventory of the china shop. What they wanted was one of farmer Jones' prize bulls to be let loose in that china shop — effectively destroying and replacing everything with something more like the AWMCC they had become accustom to. In plain speak, many American voters who voted for Obama in 2012 voted for Trump in 2016 because they had been convinced that they were about to lose their culture. They even came up with faux reasons for voting for Trump — *"Trump's a businessman and we need help with the economy"*. *"Trump will bring manufacturing jobs back home from overseas"*. And *"Trump will make America Great Again"*. All this was *"excuse speak"* for I'm voting to save white culture!

Enter Donald Trump! Trump didn't understand or know anything about the politics of governance, he was totally disrespectful of Democrats, he was uncompromising, brash, harsh, and unwavering. On the other hand, he acted as if he believed that laws were mere suggestions and that all disputes should be litigated with the party having access to the most capital (to retain legal representation the longest) being declared the winner. And what's most troubling is his inability to act presidential. He therefore resorts to his New York businessman (Mafia Don) style of leadership where everybody in his sphere (all federal employees and foreign allies) owe allegiance to him — personally.

Trump's *base*, is a mix of Tea Party left overs, Neo Nazi, Neo Confederates, Alt-Right Conservatives, prime Republican Party loyalist and White Evangelical Christian. These supporters only comprise about 22% of the electorate but they control the majority of the Republican caucus in the all-important Republican primary elections. Their weapon is a *noun gone verb* — **"Primary"**. If you're a Republican office-holder with plans to run for reelection, this word conjures up nightmare visions of defeat. Without the *base* on your side, you cannot win a Republican primary election. So, you do what you're told, or else.

This is what the **"real majority"** in the United States of American is facing today. And the Electoral College is playing an active role in the continuance of this fiasco. I believe we need to change the Electoral College in order to save America. So when Val asked me to pen a few lines about this book, its meaning, and its importance, I couldn't say no. This is *must reading* if you're an American who cares about our country. This is a *must read* even if you're not an American, but nonetheless cares about democracy and fairness, and this is a *must read* if you want peace and harmony in our ever-shrinking world.

PREFACE

If the Electoral College were eliminated tomorrow, and replaced by the popular vote, all of America's electoral and representation problems would not disappear, but Americans would have a fairer and more democratic political system.

Val Atkinson and Wayne Goodwin, Chairman — NC Democratic Party

"Val Atkinson Photos"

I began gathering materials to write this book shortly after the 2000 presidential election revealed that Vice President Al Gore was the popular vote winner in the general election for president, but Texas Governor George W. Bush *(who placed second behind Vice President Gore)* would be crowned the winner and 43rd president of the United States of America. Earlier, in the 1996 general election for president, Senator Bob Dole *(who placed second behind Bill Clinton)* did not win the election and was not crowned the 43rd president of the United States. Of course I knew why the election turned out the way it did;

but I wanted to lay things bare as would probably be done by a political novice, or someone unfamiliar with the American Electoral College system. George W. Bush won and Bob Dole lost their respective races after both had finished second. Some say that the Electoral College system should be called the *"Runner-up to the winner system, or how the loser becomes the winner system"*.

Some love the system the way it is, some *(including yours truly)* think that we outgrew the Electoral College system when we abolished slavery. And still others like the system because conservative presidential candidates don't have to campaign in states like New York, and California. These two states are considered unwinnable for conservative candidates due to the overwhelming number of progressives and liberals that reside in New York and California. Over the past few presidential elections, these two states have been prohibitively losable for conservatives and thereby losses for the Republican party.

George W. Bush entered the final days leading up to the 2000 presidential election thinking that he would win the popular vote and Al Gore might win the Electoral College. And many believe today that had the Florida vote count been allowed to continued, Al Gore would have won both. Bush was awarded the election by the U.S. Supreme Court when the court agreed with the plaintiff GOP that the vote count should be terminated. I knew then and there, that we had to do something about the Electoral College if we wanted to save our democracy. I knew that it would become increasingly difficult to explain to voters in the prohibitive states of New York, California, Wyoming, Mississippi and Montana how their individual vote mattered as much as individual votes in Pennsylvania, Florida, and North Carolina … because they don't!

The average American believes that in casting their individual vote, they control the actions of their government through their elected representatives. And that's the intent — the *de jure,* or intended process for governing our political operations. However, the *de facto* or actual process governing our political operations aren't very democratic. Only 54.2 % of eligible voters voted in the 2000 presidential election, and that figure only represented 38% of the people living in the country. In the 2016 general election for president, just 77,000 voters, or .0003% of the electorate changed the political trajectory of the country for decades still to come. All this happened while 82,000,000 voters stayed home and declined their opportunity to participate in the electoral process. The three states responsible for delivering the 77,000 votes that carried Donald J. Trump to victory were Wisconsin, Michigan and Pennsylvania.

The business of qualified voting had an inauspicious beginning in America. In 1779 (*the first election*) only white male property owners could vote. This means that the difference between the percentage of qualified voters and the percentage of actual voters was much larger in 2000 than in 1779. Things are not getting better. Most people in the country don't vote in presidential elections, but we boast about being the world's greatest democracy. We Gerrymander congressional and state legislative districts, we know that voter suppression is running rampant in almost every state (*but particularly in southern states, and states with high populations and large percentages of voters of color*). We allow the purging of voter registration files, even after receiving reports of massive wrongful purging from the roles of democrat registered voters and black and brown unaffiliated voters. And, under the guise of protected free speech, we allow lies to permeate our airwaves, and with the enactment of *Citizens United,* we allow *"Dark Money"* from wealthy individuals and corporations to literally *buy* candidates, and therefore, buy elections. And with the *gutting* of the 1965 Voting Rights Act there is no control over those who choose to dismantle our democracy — and yet, and still… we declare ourselves *"The World's Greatest Democracy".* All these things are problematic; and although changes to the Electoral College would by no means be a panacea for these problems; changes to the Electoral College system would go a long way toward resolving some of these problems and move us closer to actually being the greatest democracy in the world, both *de jure,* ***and*** *de facto.*

It's also very interesting how the state of Wyoming, with its 582,000 residents would carry as much weight as California (*with its 40,000,000 residents*) if we had a *"Contentious Election".*

The immediate political ramifications for changing the Electoral College are enormous. Currently candidates don't campaign in states they are almost assured to win or lose. They mostly campaign in what has become known as *"Battleground States".* But under a national popular vote paradigm, all votes count equally and candidates would likely spend time where the votes are … large metropolitan areas in high population states. States like California and New York will be swamped with campaign workers, and places like Somersworth, New Hampshire may not know there's an election being held. And the identification of battleground states can change over the course of an election. Michigan may be perceived as a battleground state at the beginning of a campaign, and work and resources by both campaigns could throw Michigan into the prohibitively winnable category for one of the campaigns, causing both campaigns to move resources to a more competitive state.

The other issue not lost in considering changes to the Electoral College system is the demographic and ethnic composition of the large metropolitan areas and small towns. People of color in this country are primarily concentrated in large metropolitan areas. The African American population in New York City alone is more than the combined population of the states of *Wyoming, Montana, South Dakota, and North Dakota.* This also means that the African American vote in New York is equal to about 4 of New York's 29 electoral college votes; whereas the total electoral college vote of the 4 aforementioned states (none having more than 1% African American population) is 12. Plainly put, 2 million African Americans have 4 votes and less than 2 million whites have 12 votes … go figure.

When Article II was being debated regarding the method to select the leader of the country, southern states were not comfortable with an election system that would allow northern, non-slaveholding states to out-vote them and challenge the institution of slavery. So, they agreed on a system that would be weighted towards slaveholding states. {*Less we forget, the population of the United States in 1780 was less than 4 million people including slaves — which out-numbered whites in many southern states. And even as late as the beginning of the Civil War the U.S. population was only 31* million}. But now that legal slavery has ended, do we still need the Electoral College to protect the voting rights of slaveholding plantation owners? In 1787 we needed a system for electing the president that all could agree on. In 1800, 1824, 1836, 1872, 1876, 1888, 2000, and 2016 we learned that the Electoral College system is not without its faults. So, the question arises, *"**when and how do we fix it?**"*

With the country being polarized on the question of totally eliminating the Electoral College, a constitutional amendment is almost out of the question due to the requirement of having two-thirds votes in both chambers of the congress (288 votes in the House of Representatives and 67 votes in the U.S. Senate) and a three-fourths vote of the various legislatures (38 states). But the NPVIC (National Popular Vote Interstate Compact) shows promise.

Whether we modify the current Electoral College process with the NPVIC or some other system, we must address the circumstances that produce such inequities in our electoral system that permit the outcomes we experienced in 2000 and 2016. We are moving in the wrong direction if we are interested in becoming the De facto greatest democracy in the world.

Being the greatest democracy in the world doesn't mean being the greatest military or economic might in the world who happens to profess democracy. It means being the greatest *practitioner* of democracy in the world ... and we're not there yet.

The Electoral College's impact on the equal protection of all votes, irrespective of race, ethnicity or region of the country is an on-going major concern.

The assault on the black vote actually began in 1870, immediately after the ratification of the 15ᵗʰ Amendment — which gave black men the vote. During slavery, southern slaveholding states were over represented in the U.S. House of Representatives due to the *3/5 clause* which counted all slaves as 3/5 of a person for the purpose of Congressional Apportionment in the U.S. House of Representatives. After the passage of the 14ᵗʰ Amendment those persons that were counted as 3/5 of a person could be counted as whole persons. This act alone increased the south's congressional representation by 20%. The obvious solution to this conundrum was to accept the added numbers that counting former slaves as whole persons would bring to their state, while simultaneously denying blacks the vote. The creative genius that went into creating laws and policy to deny the franchise to black men was striking. For every *"Tit"* established by the Freedmen's Bureau, there was the proverbial *"Tat"* by the various southern states — led by the states of Mississippi and South Carolina.

So we find ourselves today in a paradox where the defeated south still throws her weight around. The south first captured the Democrats to *"tote their water"* then they switched to the Republican party when the Democrats began backing desegregation and allowing black people to register and vote. And now it is argued by some that the GOP is literally owned by the white south. They (the GOP) dare not embrace any policy or position that could remotely appear to benefit people of color without risking the loss of the white vote in the former Confederate states. It is therefore highly problematic for Republicans to attract black voters. The GOP by nature *must* fall on the side of the white southern position in all respects — even when doing so alienates blacks and other people of color. So, one might ask, how do Republicans tackle this mammoth problem? The answer is obviously *"change"*, and the first step is to change the Electoral College.

INTRODUCTION

North Carolina State Capitol Building

"Val Atkinson Photos"

This book reveals the open-face inequities and anti-democratic tenets of the Electoral College. It lays bare the reasons for the establishment of the Electoral College, and it also illuminates the confusion and complications inherent in the system still today. It spells-out clearly how the system is not good for minority voters, and it offers solutions to our current system of electoral maladies.

Could this be why no other country on the planet has attempted to replicate the Electoral College system in their country? Could it be that none of the 50 states nor the District of Columbia have decided to implemented an Electoral College system because it's not a good system?

In the first chapter of this book the foundation for the ensuing arguments are clearly outlined regarding the need to eliminate or change the Electoral College system. Two polls *(one by MorningConsult.com and the other conducted by this book)* clearly cite the need for a hard look at our current electoral system and why it should be modified or replaced. It was striking to learn that large swaths of our electorate don't know how their leaders are elected, let alone, *why and how* they are elected as they are. The polls indicate that very small sections of our overall population are determining who gets to be considered for elective office, and thereby setting the stage for the ultimate winner.

Long before we had a nation, a constitution, or the twelfth amendment, there was a desire among colonist to avoid dictators and tyrants and gravitate towards justice, equality, and democracy. This was due to how the colonist were treated by the ruling British. After the British formally recognized their former colonies as a sovereign nation — the United States of America, this new country didn't yet know what kind of government it wanted. But they knew unequivocally that they didn't want a monarchical dictatorship. They ultimately settled on a president. The problem came when they tried to decide how the president would be chosen. The recommendations of the Committee of Eleven settled that problem when they recommended that we establishment the Electoral College. They also considered selecting the president by state legislatures, by governors or *(God forbid)* by the people. Whether we needed the Electoral College then or not is a moot point, but whether or not we need it now is a question to be pondered. First of all, it can be argued that we're as polarized now as we've ever been as a nation — and it getting worse. In 1787 the framers didn't have to deal with minority voting rights because minorities couldn't vote; only white male property owners could vote. But now we have the 12th, 13th, 14th, 15th, 17th, 19th, 20th, 22nd, 23rd, and 26th Amendments. They all have to do (in some measure) with electing the president. Ten of the 17 amendments passed after the "Bill of Rights" have to do with election rights in some form or another. We've amended the constitution 27 times and we don't have it right yet. What we need is a 28th Amendment that does to the 12th Amendment, what the 21st Amendment did for the 18th Amendment — *repeal it!*

Additionally, since 1932 African Americans have increasingly gravitated to the Democratic Party. This was due in part to Roosevelt's

New Deal in the 1930's. Later came Truman's desegregation order as one of the planks in the Democratic Platform of 1948 which was followed by the Brown Decision in 1954, and the Civil Rights Act in 1964. So by the time the Voting Rights Act was passed in 1965 African Americans were strongly tethered to the Democratic Party — having left their original party of Lincoln, the GOP.

Because African Americans vote over-whelmingly for Democrat candidates, the GOP took advantage of this fact and embraced the *"Southern Strategy"* that sealed the white southern vote for GOP candidates — the polarization became worse. So where we find ourselves now is in a political election model that has *"Race"* written all over it. And now may be the time to solve two or more issues with one cure. We need desperately to change the Electoral College so that race can't be used as a mitigating factor to elect the President of the United States.

Some say that because we're all Americans it doesn't matter who wins — I say it does. It matters because as much as we like to think we have a political system that ensures equality of opportunity, all Americans aren't equal, and they don't have the same opportunities. So, when we look at *"Citizens United" "Shelby v Holder",* and *Rucho v Common Cause,* we see that the equality is not there and won't be anytime soon. This has been compounded by Senator Mitch McConnell's refusal to consider Merrick Brian Garland for the Supreme Court and disregarding his given reason for the non-consideration of Garland and rushing Amy Coney Barrett's nomination through the hearing process. This was as brazen as it could get. It's especially brazen due to the long term impact of justice Barrett's placement on the highest court of the land. What these three rulings and senate chicanery did to the American electoral system borders on the criminal. Citizen United allows corporations and wealthy individuals to literally purchase elections by using their enormous money piles to buy-off would-be antagonist from seeking public office. They hire lobbyist to write bills for Congresspersons to introduce and vote on. In return they finance the campaigns of these Congresspersons and let them know unequivocally that if they ever stray from the present ideology, they can expect truck-loads of campaign contributions to be forwarded to their opponent in the next election.

This is frightening for a congressperson who has to run for reelection every two years.

In Shelby *v.* Holder the Court struck-down Section 4 of the 1965 Voting Rights Act. Section 4 was the engine that made the Voting Rights Act go. Section 4 determine which states or portions of states would come under the auspices of the Act and required *"preclearance"* before any changes to voting procedures could be enacted. Without the requirement of preclearance, many states (led by Pennsylvania, Texas and North Carolina) rushed to establish restrictions that had little or no chance of being implemented if it were not for the Shelby *v.* Holder ruling striking down Section 4 of the 1965 Voting Rights Act. In June of 2019 the courts struck voters once again. This time it was Gerrymandering, but once again it was still North Carolina. In *Rucho v Common Cause* the court ruled that political Gerrymandering was *OK,* and that voters could vote the lawmakers out of office if they didn't like the way they were Gerrymandering their districts. My question to the court was, how do voters vote them out, when your ruling has given legislators permission to legally *choose their own voters?*

The first concern we should have about the Electoral College is its weight towards smaller states. Smaller states received their first weighting with the Connecticut plan which gave us a bi-cameral government with one of the houses having equal representation for all states, regardless of size. The second weighting was with *Article I, Section 2, Clause 3;* the 3/5 provision that allowed slaveholding states with small white populations to count their slaves to gain greater representation in the lower house. This grew even greater after the enactment of the 14th Amendment in 1868, which counted slaves as full persons — giving these states more representation in the House of Representatives without increasing their white populations. But the weighting of the Electoral College is minimal when compared with the fact that when the Electoral College meets and votes, the people would have already voted all over the country and rendered their choice for President and Vice President. If we're really a country of, and for the people, why is it necessary for a group of 538 non-elected citizens (electors) to have the final say as to whom will lead us for the next four years?

Equally disturbing is the fact that Americans know very little about the Electoral College and how it's used to determine the winner of the presidential election. According to the results of polls discussed in chapter I, Americans between 18 and 29 know least about the Electoral College and those between the ages of 51 and 75 are most knowledgeable. In the demographic of race, Whites scored highest and Latinos scored lowest. African Americans scored slightly ahead of Latinos. Females fared much better than males and Independents topped the list in the Political Party category. Moderates led the way in Ideology, and as expected, those with advanced degrees top the polls in Education. The states with the highest average were as follows: Washington, Massachusetts, Connecticut, California, New York, Maryland, Virginia, District of Columbia, Minnesota, and Iowa. On the other end of the scale were: Kentucky, West Virginia, Mississippi, Arkansas, Alabama, Louisiana, Missouri, South Carolina, Tennessee, and Idaho. Voting history indicated that those who voted regularly far out-paced those who were irregular voters or those yet to vote.

Crosstabs were even more interesting. A few surprises were: Black males over 75 knew more about the Electoral College that white females under 30, and those checking the "none" option under religion did far better than those checking the Jewish or Islamic categories.

The answer to the question, *"How does the Electoral College works?"* is not as important as the answer to the question *"Why do we still have it?"*. But to intelligently take a position that the college should be eliminated or modified, one should know what the consequences and advantages are. So, the short answer is that the Electoral College is a multifaceted, complicated, archaic political system whose initial purpose has been served and needs to be reexamined under today's optics using today's measurements, social norms, populations, and technologies.

We must correct the Electoral College before it politically destroys us all.

CHAPTER I

What the public knows and doesn't know about the Electoral College

*A*fter reviewing *Morning Consult's National Tracking Poll # 190346, conducted March 22-24, 2019,* the answer to the burning question … *"Do we know enough about the Electoral College to make intelligent decisions regarding its retention and/or modification?"*, is a resounding **NO!**

I have included some of the salient points of the survey in this portion of the book, and I invite readers to review the poll in its entirety courtesy *www.MorningConsult.com*.

Methodology:

National Tracking Poll #190346 March 22-24, 2019

Cross Tabulation Results

This poll was conducted between March 22 and March 24, 2019 among a national sample of 1994 Registered Voters. Interviews were conducted online and the data were weighted to approximate a target sample of Registered Voters based on age, educational attainment, gender, race, and region. Results from the full survey have a margin of error of plus or minus 2 percentage points.

Crosstab demographics included:

Gender
Age
Political I.D.
Ideology
Education
Income
Ethnicity
Religion
Community
Employment
Military
Direction of Country
Trump's Job Approval
Regions of Residence
Voting History

Issues

— *Economy*
— *Security*
— *Health Care*
— *Medicare / Social Security*
— *Women's Issues*
— *Education*
— *Energy*
— *Other*

In table POL5_5 respondents were queried about their knowledge of Elizabeth Warren's remarks concerning the elimination of the Electoral College. Then they were asked if they knew how our president was elected. They were further asked if the president should be elected by the Electoral College or by National Popular Vote. The next question was a little more difficult. The question asked about their knowledge of the

NPVIC or National Popular Vote Interstate Compact. They then were asked whether the Electoral College should remain, considering that it sometime allows the loser of the popular vote to become president. The answers to these questions by the various demographic were very interesting and may shed great light on the impending general election of 2020

Age — The segment of the age demographic with the highest percentage of respondents checking *"a lot or some"* was the age group of 65 and older. Sixty-five percent of respondents in this age category responded that they had heard or seen a lot or some having to do with Elizabeth Warren remark about eliminating the Electoral College. The age group of 18 – 29 responded that their age group had seen or heard the least about Senator Warren's Electoral College remarks. This is remarkable because the youth vote will be instrumental in any attempt to modify or eliminate the Electoral College.

Gender — In the demographic of gender males appeared to have won the battle of the sexes when it came to being aware of the U.S. Senator's remarks about the Electoral College.

Political — Politically, Democrats bested Republicans by 3 percentage points. But this difference should have been greater due to the party affiliation of Senator Warren, which is Democrat.

Ideological — Liberals appeared to been more aware of Warren's stance than their conservative counterparts. But this is expected as well, in that Senator Warren is widely considered to lean much more liberal than conservative.

Education — There was a 24 % spread (70% and 46 %) between those respondents with post-graduate degrees and those with less than a bachelor's degree that had heard or seen something about Warren's position on the Electoral College. This could prove to be problematic as well.

Income — Sixty-four percent of those earning $100,000.00 per year or more responded that they had heard or seen something about Warren's position. The sub-category of income that had the least exposure to Warren's position was the category of people that earned less than $50,000.00 per year.

ETHNICITY — Here we find a disturbing trend. Fifty-six percent of whites, and fifty-six percent of Hispanics had seen or heard of Warren's position, while only forty-eight percent of African Americans had seen or heard what a progressive (some say liberal) female Democratic Senator from Massachusetts had said about the Elector College, when many say (yours truly included) that the Electoral College is not good for Black and Brown voters *(see more in chapter VI)*.

Religion — Catholics and Protestants scored relatively equal in the responses from this demographic. Sixty-one percent of Catholics and sixty percent of Protestants responded that they had heard a lot or some about Senator Warren's positon on the Electoral College.

Community — Suburban respondents scored highest when compared with Urban and Rural respondents. This is an expected outcome when other demographics such as education, income, and voting age participation are examined. Suburban residents have the highest income, highest education and participate in the voting process more frequently than other community demographics. It is therefore expected that they would have heard or seen more about Senator Warren's position on the Electoral College than the other two demographics would **have**.

Employment — The results from this category was somewhat surprising. The category with the highest awareness of Senator Warren's position was expected *(retired persons)* but the demographic with the lowest awareness was surprising *(students)*.

How does the United States elect its president? — Seventy-three percent of all respondents said the president was elected by the electoral college. But this was a multiple-choice format. If this would have been an essay reply format the results may not have been as high. The breakdown by ethnicity, community and employment were as follows:

Community

Suburban	73%
Urban	77%
Rural	65%

Ethnicity

White	76%
Hispanic	63%
Black	56%

Employment

Students	64% *(lowest)*

African Americans and students appears to be less informed about exactly how our president is elected. This could prove to be problematic when we consider that those whom the Electoral College impacts most negatively know least about it.

Would you prefer the Electoral College or the National Popular Vote? — A plurality of men favored the National Popular Vote or the Electoral College, but women favored the National Popular Vote overwhelming, 53 – 24. The only demographics that preferred the Electoral College over the National Popular Vote were conservatives, Republicans, and Trump supporters.

Which of the two would you prefer (Electoral College or NPVIC *(National Popular Vote Interstate Compact)*?

Income over $100,000.00 annually	*45-42 — Electoral College*
Protestants	*47-35 — Electoral College*
Non-Evangelical Catholics	*51-30 — Electoral College*
All Christians	*41-39 — Electoral College*
Trump Supporters	*41-39 — Electoral College*

Which of the two would you prefer (Keep EC or Constitutional Amendment)?

Men	*70-23 — Keep Electoral College*
Protestants	*48-39 — Keep Electoral College*
Catholics	*51-38 — Keep Electoral College*
Rural	*42-41 — Keep Electoral College*

ANALYSIS

My analysis of the data in this poll was done by combining the positive responses (*"a lot, and some"*) and contrasting them against the combined negative responses (*"not much and nothing at all"*).

On the question of whether they preferred the Electoral College or the National Popular Vote to determine the election of the president, the results were clear.

Both male and female preferred the National Popular Vote over the Electoral College (females favored the National Popular Vote over the Electoral College more so than their male counterparts — *male 46-42, female 53-27*). The only demographics that preferred the Electoral College over the National Popular vote were: *Republicans, Trump supporters, and conservatives of either party.*

When comparing the Electoral College with the NPVIC (National Popular Vote Interstate Compact) several demographics preferred the Electoral College over the NPVIC. They were: *Respondents with incomes over $100,000.00 annually, Protestants, Non-Evangelicals, Catholics, All Christians, and Trump supporters.*

When comparing Keeping the Electoral College as is, or changing it with a constitutional amendment, the results were striking: The following demographics did not want a constitutional amendment to replace the Electoral College: *Protestants, Catholics, Rural residents, all non-Christians, and all men.*

Without drawing a hard conclusion, I have pointed-out several responses that bare greater opining. First is the positive correlation between older respondents and knowledge of the Electoral College system. Many political observers take the position that our senior population has fewer distractions and therefore become more politically engaged as they age. I don't totally discount this theory on its face, but would offer a competing theory as well. My contention is that seniors, over the age of 65, became politically aware/motivated during the Civil Rights and Vietnam War eras. All politics were personal in the 1960's and 1970's. If you were African American, *you were* the Civil Rights Movement, and the Civil Rights Movement *was you*. And if you were white you knew someone that had been drafted, was serving in Vietnam, or was on their way there. If you were in the media, your lead story every night was about civil rights, race relations, or the Vietnam war.

And of course, there were the assassinations and killings: *1963 – President John F. Kennedy, 1963 – Ku Klux Klan bombing in Birmingham, Alabama, 1963 – Medgar Evers shot in the back in his carport, 1964 – Goodman, Schwerner, and Chaney murdered in Philadelphia, Mississippi because that were there to help black Mississippians register to vote, 1965 – Malcomb X murdered in New York, 1965 – Viola Liuzzo (a white woman) murdered while driving a black man in Neshoba County, Mississippi, 1968 – Martin Luther King assassinated in Memphis, Tennessee, 1968 – Robert Kennedy assassinated in California, 1969 – Fred Hampton murdered by police.*

Each assassination and killing had a profound impact on my personal politics. My political ideology was cast in the civil rights era of the 50's, 60's, and 70's. In the mid 50's my fears were stoked by the Emmitt Till murder, but my aspirations were buoyed by Rosa Parks and the Rev. Dr. Martin Luther King Jr. and the bus boycott in Montgomery, Alabama. This added to the crowning decision of the 50's — the Supreme Court ruling that reversed *Plessey v Ferguson* and declared "separate but equal" was unconstitutional. The *Brown v Board of Education* decision was a sea change in race relations in America. The killing of the four little girls in Birmingham, the assassination of Medgar Evers, the brutal murders of Goodman, Chaney and Schwerner, the senseless killing of Viola Liuzzo, and the time stopping political assassination of Martin

Luther King were all in retaliation for the *Brown v Board of Education* decision in 1954.

In the 50's 60's and 70's we learned that we were politics and politics was us. I'm not so sure that Gen "Xers" and Millennials have been equally motivated politically. Although we had distractions as well (R&B groups, sports heroes, and Hippies) most of us managed to stay focused on the target at hand — politics. And although the target has morphed, moved, and changed in so many ways, even now in the autumn of our years we are still focused on the target at hand. And whether we call it boycotting or selective purchasing; marches & rallies or town hall meetings; walking the neighborhood and door-knocking or trolling the internet, it's all the same, just done in a different era under a different name.

So, what this survey response tells me is ... ***"our young folks got some work to do!"*** and for that matter, so does our communities of color, low wealth and diminished education attainment. I therefore decided to conduct a survey in areas with concentrations of people of varying ethnicity with low wealth and low to moderate education attainment. This is what I found.

Random Electoral College Survey

Conducted by
The Electoral College and the Black and Brown Vote

Methodology:

The survey was conducted over a period of two months (August 1, 2019 through September 30, 2019). This was a "take home" survey, and respondents were encouraged to research questions. A total of 641 subjects responded to this survey.

Survey Questions:

1. When was the Electoral College established?
   a. 1787
   b. 1789
   c. 1804
   d. 1954

2. How many electors is your state authorized? _____.

3. How are Governors and U.S. Senators elected?
   a. By Electoral College vote
   b. By Congressional Districts
   c. By Statewide popular vote
   d. By State Legislatures

4. How are members of the U.S. House of Representatives selected?
   a. By Statewide Popular vote
   b. By Congressional District vote
   c. By Gubernatorial Appointment
   d. By State Legislative Appointment

5. How many electors comprise the Electoral College?
   a. 50
   b. 51
   c. 435
   d. 538

6. Which state has the most Electoral College votes?
    a. Wyoming
    b. New York
    c. California
    d. Texas

7. When does the Electoral College vote?
    a. The Tuesday after the first Monday in November
    b. The Tuesday after the first Wednesday in December
    c. The Monday after the third Wednesday in December
    d. The Monday after the second Wednesday in December

8. For whom does the Electoral College vote?
    a. U.S. Senate leaders
    b. Leaders in the U.S. House of Representatives
    c. The President and the Supreme Court
    d. The President and Vice President

9. How are electors selected?
    a. Appointed by the governor
    b. By state legislatures
    c. Appointed by the various political parties
    d. By popular vote

10. Are electors required to vote as they pledge to vote?
    a. Yes
    b. No

11. After the Civil War the Electoral College gave enormous election advantages to the south.
    a. True
    b. False

12. Which Amendment(s) had an impact on dthe Electoral College?
    a. 12th Amendment
    b. 13th Amendment

    c. 14ᵗʰ Amendment

    d. 15ᵗʰ Amendment

    e. 19ᵗʰ Amendment

    f. 23ʳᵈ Amendment

    g. 26ᵗʰ Amendment

    h. All of the above

13. What are Faithless Electors?
    a. Electors without religious affiliations
    b. Electors without political affiliations
    c. Electors who vote differently than they pledged to vote
    d. Electors who refuse compensation for their services

14. How old were you when you first learned that there was an Electoral College? _____.

15. What are contentious elections?
    a. Elections that are too close to call
    b. Elections that have more than one winner
    c. Elections that produced no winner
    d. Elections that produced great discourse

16. How many votes are needed to win in the Electoral College?
    a. 538
    b. 435
    c. 270
    d. 101

17. In which geographical section of the country does most African Americans reside?
    a. Northeast
    b. West Coast
    c. South
    d. Midwest

18. In the last five presidential elections, which geographical section of the country cast the greatest number of Electoral College votes for the Republican party candidate?
    a. Northeast
    b. West Coast
    c. South
    d. Midwest

19. What is the "Unit" method of Electoral College vote distribution?
    a. Each candidate gets an equal share of all votes cast
    b. The popular vote winner takes all the votes
    c. Each candidate only gets those votes that were cast for him/her.
    d. Each candidate gets one "Unit" for every Electoral College vote cast for him.

20. Which of the following is correct?
    a. Most Americans would like to see presidents elected by a national popular vote.
    b. Maine and Nebraska practice a proportional method of Electoral College vote distribution.
    c. Both A and B are correct
    d. Neither a. nor b. is correct

21. *I researched or was assisted with the survey questions.*
    a. *True*
    b. *False*

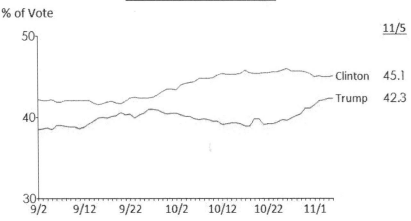

National Poll Average

% of Vote

11/5

Clinton 45.1

Trump 42.3

Survey Results Analysis

The average survey response score was 45 out of a possible 100. This confirms my hypothesis that most Americans don't understand the system they use to elect their leaders. Some of the outstanding revelations were: Less than 15% of respondents were aware that most African Americans reside in the south and that the south is the geographical section that cast most votes for Republicans, although the region is considerably outnumbered by the northeast section of the country. This was significant and is discussed in greater detail in chapter VI.

DEMOGRAPHIC ANALYSIS

AGE – *Group 51-75* scored highest overall. This comports with another of my hypothesis that seniors pay more attention to political activities than their younger counterparts. Not surprising, the age group with the lowest average score was the 18-29 year old group. Here, my response is in the form of a question. I wonder if, *(beyond the obvious lack of detailed interest on social media sites)* Millennials see the direct connect between voting, democracy and freedom that out seniors experienced while growing up during World War II, the Korean Conflict, and Vietnam.

Or maybe it's the competition the seniors didn't experience from *"Swing Music in the '40's, Pop and Jazz in the '50's and Soul and Rock in the '60's and '70's.* Maybe today's *Hip-Hop culture* is a little too strong to resist. And just maybe, it's crowding out some of the things youngsters were in tune to decades ago ... just maybe. But I digress.

RACE – *The Group African American or Black* scored lowest of all the racial groups listed. The reasoning for this result escapes me with the exception of the segregated housing patterns still persistent in the United States of America today. And it's common knowledge that housing patterns determine the quality of schools in our public education system; and the less affluent housing sections produce lower quality schools, which in turn produces students that don't do well on Val Atkinson's Electoral College Survey. White respondents had the highest group average in this category.

GENDER – *The Group Male* scored highest of these two choices. But the difference was not significant. Females had the highest median score, while males had the highest mean score.

POLITICAL PARTY – *The Group Non-Affiliated* scored highest in the political party category. It would be difficult to confirm that party affiliation determined one's intelligence, or that smarter people gravitated towards a particular party, however, the category of education does show that Democrats have a considerably higher mean score than their competing parties. Non-affiliates have increased in numbers recently due to Democrats and Republicans becoming disenchanted with their party but refuse to register with their main opposition.

IDEOLOGY – *The Group Progressive* scored highest in the ideology category. The range from highest to lowest was as follows: Progressive, Liberal, Moderate and Conservative. This finding seems to suggest that ideology alone does not determine one's knowledge base, political leaning or insight. But when we hold for education we find that lower educated progressives and liberals didn't do as well as higher educated moderates and conservatives. In this case education wins out over ideology. Maybe that's the way it should be

EDUCATION – *The Group Advanced Degree* scored highest in the education category. There were no surprises here.

INCOME – *The Group 51-75* scored highest here. Here too, (with the exception of the over 100K group) education plays a role in determining the outcome for this category. For the most part, there's always been a positive correlation between education attained and income earned; so these results did not surprise us either.

ETHNICITY — *The Group White* scored highest in this category. This was expected due to the history of suppressed educational opportunities in this country. African Americans and Latinos did not fair well in this survey. It is discussed further in the conclusions section.

RELIGION — *The Group Christians* scored highest in this category. America is predominantly Christian country, and other religions are not represented in high numbers in this or many other random surveys. It was notable that the very small Jewish population that responded to the survey scored very high on the survey.

STATE — *There was a significant number of respondents that chose not to respond to this portion of the survey. Of the Respondents that chose to respond, the respondents from Maryland scored highest. Maryland was followed by the District of Columbia, New York and Pennsylvania. These four states scored in the 1st quintile. States scoring in the 5th quintile were Florida, Georgia, South Carolina, and North Carolina.*

COMMUNITY — *The Group Suburban* scored significantly higher than the categories of urban, rural and exurbs.

EMPLOYMENT — *The Group Retired* scored highest in this category, and surprisingly, students fell to 3rd behind employed. Unemployed scored fourth.

MILITARY SERVICE — *This Binary Selection* revealed that those respondents with military service backgrounds were outscored by those that chose not to serve in our military ranks.

VOTING HISTORY — *The Group Regular Voter* scored highest in this category, and survey results from respondents who were not eligible to vote were not tallied in the final results of the survey.

SURVEY ASSISTANCE — *Only 37% of respondents sought or received survey assistance.*

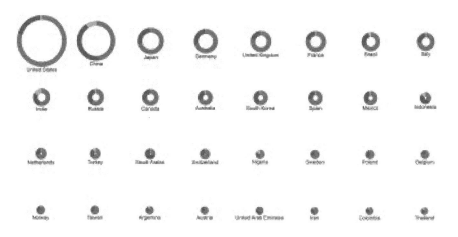

Significant Crosstabs

If we would try to clone a person from the survey data received it would be something that no one recognizes. The combined data suggest that the person most knowledgeable about the Electoral College System and the Electoral Process that supports it, is: *A white male in his 60's, a Non-Affiliated Voter with Progressive leanings, holds a graduate degree but only earns between 50 and 75 thousand dollars annually, practices the Christian religion, lives in the suburb surrounding one of the major cities of the state of Maryland, is retired and a non-veteran.*

On the other end of the spectrum we have a registered Republican who believes in a conservative ideology, is a non-high school graduate, is an unemployed veteran and happens to be a young black female. When she works she earns less than 35 thousand per year, and she lives in one of the urban centers in the state of North Carolina.

Again, it's confusing, most of us have never met such a person. But this is what the survey data tells us. So, for clarification purposes, we decided to cherry-pick some of the crosstabs in an attempt to shed more plausible light on the matter.

Those scoring highest on the survey were white males in their 60's. This should come as no surprise. We could give this group any survey or test involving any aspect of American history, governmental operations, or basic civics and they would do very well. This group of citizens, also known as *"Baby Boomers"* were educated under a different system than were the other cohorts in our survey. The expectations were different, the curriculum was different, the teachers were different, and the overall culture was different. So, quite naturally the outcomes should be expected to be different.

Back in the day, family members actually ate together; and while eating they *talked* to each other (they weren't all tethered to their electronic devices). Subsequently they learned from each other as well as from their formal education. They became inquisitive to the extent that they became involved in research that resulted in serendipitous learning as well. Unfortunately that type of *"Back-in-the-Day"* learning doesn't take place as often today, and we're **not** better-off because of it.

The message portrayed by the results of these surveys is very clear ... *Americans are unfamiliar with the system they use to elect their leader — the President of the United States of America.* The dearth of basic operational knowledge of the Electoral College is astounding. This begs the question, *"Do we really have a democracy, or are we fooling ourselves?"* If so many of us don't understand the system under which we live, why are we asking more questions and demanding more clarity? Maybe the answer is in the old adage about the ox ... *"It all depends on whose ox is being gored"*. The present day construct of the Electoral College clearly favors smaller states and states with over-representation of white voters due to Voter Suppression and Gerrymandering. Those supporters of the Electoral College that live in the mountain west and southern states are well aware that if the Electoral College were replaced by the popular vote (if we let the people select the president and vice president) conservative, GOP candidates would have little chance of winning.

To put it in other terms … let's suppose that a civil war between rival factions in a sub Saharan nation ended by having both factions recognized as separate sovereign states by the United Nations. The condition for recognition was that the people would determine the form of government they lived under by voting for their choice of government. If one of the factions only allowed registered Communist to vote, would we say this was a fair election and that the results represented the will of the people?

The Founding Fathers

CHAPTER II

How The Electoral College Got Started

It appears that one of the founders was more involved in the establishment of the Electoral College than history has led us to believe. James Wilson of North Carolina (by way of Pennsylvania and Scotland) had a special hand in the 3/5 rule and the Elector College.

James Wilson

In 1787, when the Constitutional Convention was held in Philadelphia, Pennsylvania, the drafters of the Constitution became weary that smaller states and slaveholding states might bolt if provisions were not installed in the Constitution that would protect their **"RIGHTS"** to **"OWN"** other human beings, while at the same time professing to establish a constitution that would protect the rights of all to pursue happiness, freedom and justice.

What has now come to be known as the framers met on May 25, 1787; ostensibly to revise and complete issues arising from discussions and plans to institute a *"League of States"* under the *"Articles of Confederation"*. But Alexander Hamilton of New York and James Madison of Virginia had different plans. These two framers were interested in enacting an entirely new system ... *"THE CONSTITUTION OF THE UNITED STATES OF AMERICA"*.

Article I's largest hurdle was what type of legislature we would have — *A body based on population or a body based on equal representation of the states.* The Connecticut plan introduced by Robert Sherman (of Connecticut) that suggested that we have a bicameral legislature with the lower house elected by population and the upper house elected by equal representation won the day. Once that hurdle was cleared it was on to Article II (the executive branch). The great question here wasn't what type of leader should we install, but how should we install him. Several ideas arose — *Direct Elections, Election by Governors, Appointment by the Legislature, Election by the Legislature, or Election by Electors appointed by the various states.*

After several weeks of obfuscation, wrangling, and deal making everybody was anxious to get home in time for harvest season. They wanted to adjourn with all the states intact. So, in effect, coming up with a deal that satisfied everyone about how the chief executive was to be elected became critically important. They tried their best, but their best wasn't good enough. Their voting was all over the map of choices from Direct Elections by the people to Elections by Electors.

Direct Elections were deemed untenable because they thought that the country was so spread-out and unnavigable that candidates would not be able to become known outside their home states rendering the direct elections a battle of *"Favorite Sons"*. All states would vote for the candidate they know best, giving candidates from larger states a decided advantage, and hopelessly disadvantaging candidates from rural areas. Elections by Governors didn't get very much support either. The prevailing concern was the corruption factor. Governors as singular heads of a state could have significant sway over not only their own state, but conceivably over the President of the United States.

After discussions and voting on all possible choices they ended with the least reprehensible choice — Election by Electors. Now they could all go home and harvest. But what they've left us with has become almost non-harvestable.

James Wilson played a significant role in the development of legislation that affected Africans and African Americans as well. In addition to the Three-Fifths Compromise incentivizing slave owners to buy and own more slaves for the purpose of unearned representation in the U.S. House of Representatives, it created the need to keep the Electoral College system. They knew that if they would lose the Three-Fifths Compromise they would lose representation in the House and lose their ability to protect their Peculiar Institution.

Today we find that the Electoral College is being used to benefit the former slaveholding states just as the Three-Fifths Compromise did before the Reconstruction Amendments (13th -14th -15th) were ratified. So when the Electoral College is discussed, the name of James Wilson should always be included.

Before the delegates accepted the Committee of Eleven's recommendation the following votes were taken:

May 29th	*Virginia Plan Includes Selection by national legislature*
June 2nd	*Delegates vote 2-8 against* *Delegates vote 8-2 for*
June 8th	*Delegates vote 9-2 to reconsider selection by national legislature*
June 9th	*Delegates vote 0-10 against selection by governors*
June 15th	*New Jersey Plan Calls for Selection by national legislature*
July 17th	*Delegates vote 9-1 against direct election of president*
July 19th	*Delegates vote 6-3-1 for selection of president by electors*
July 23rd	*Delegates vote 7-3 to reconsider selection by electors*
July 25th	*Delegates vote 7-4 against selection by legislature*

July 26th	*Delegates vote 7-3 for selection by national legislature*
August 6th	*Committee on Detail reports in favor of selection by national legislature*
August 24th	*Delegates reject 2-9 attempt to change from selection by national legislature to by the people*
August 31st	*Delegates cannot decide on choosing the president. Assign problem to new Committee of Eleven*
September 4th	*Committee of Eleven recommend selection by electors chosen by decision of state legislatures*
September 6th	*Delegates vote 9-2 for selection by electors*
	Change venue of Contingent election from Senate to House
	Delegates vote 8-3 for one vote per state in House contingent elections
September 7th	*Delegates approve electoral college plan for selecting president*

The voting table above clearly illustrates how contentious the process was to determine how the president was to be selected. So obviously there was great concern for keeping the union together. But should that concern be the guiding reason we retain the Electoral College today?

As of the publication date of this book, Republicans have won the popular vote once in the last seven elections or 24 years, (1992 – 2016) but have been crowned the winner "three" times (2000, 2004, and 2016). We're the only country on the planet in which this could possible happen.

James Wilson ended the Constitutional Convention by declaring that … *"This subject (the Electoral College) is in truth the most difficult of all on which we have had to decide".* He later, in December, as he addressed the legislature of his home state of Pennsylvania reaffirmed … *"The convention was perplexed with no part of this plan so much as with the mode of choosing the President of the United States".*

Over a 22 day period the convention held thirty votes before turning the process over to the Committee of Eleven. The Committee of Eleven recommended that the President be selected by Electors chosen by state legislatures — The Delegates adopted this selection method.

As in so many chapters in this book you'll find here that we aren't able to get away from the issue of race and slavery playing a key and major role in the establishment and operations of this newly found republic. From the concern of the delegates at the Constitutional Convention right through the 116th Congress the issues of equality and racial privilege are also operating just beneath the surface.

America's current fortunes were first made possible by the genocide and culturecide of the Native American population in the Western Hemisphere. Secondly, the Europeans led chiefly by the British took Johann Blumenbach's theory on racial stratification to a new height. Blumenbach theorized that the white man (because of his larger cranial size) was superior to all other races, and that the black man was intellectually inferior because of his comparative smaller sized head. European slave traders took this to another level by putting Blumenbach's theory into forced practice. Slavery was big business in the Americas, and the new United States of America wanted to keep it going to build it new economy. This meant keeping the states happy, which meant keeping the slaveholders happy. This is prima facie causation for selecting the 3/5 representation rule and the selection by electors. It's also, as George C. Edwards III would say … **"Why The Electoral College is Bad for America".**

Professor Wilfred Codrington III of New York University School of Law began his eye opening essay about the Electoral College's Racist Origins with this … *"More than two centuries after it was designed to empower southern white voters, the system continues to do just that".* He later gave his reason for this as he cited a quote from William F. Buckley, which reads … *"White Americans are entitled to take such measures as are necessary to prevail, politically and culturally anywhere they are outnumbered because they are part of the **Advanced Race".***

Codrington ends with some words that I shall never forget … **"The Nation's oldest structural racial entitlement program is one of its most consequential: THE ELECTORAL COLLEGE"**

CHAPTER III

How the Electoral College Works

Supreme Court Of The United States (SCOTUS

Courtesy Val Atkinson Photos

*G*errymandering impacts state legislatures which impact Redistricting, which impacts control over the lower house of Congress, which makes the laws, declares war, determines the budget, and decides whether to impeach the president. And if no candidate for president receives 270 electoral college votes, the U.S. House of Representatives elects the President and the U.S. Senate elects the Vice President. Under these circumstances, the state of Wyoming becomes as powerful as the state of California, each only having one vote to elect the president. Wyoming has approximately ½ million residents, while California has almost 40 *million, but when the election of the president is thrown into the House of Representatives, each state has only 1 vote regardless of the size of the state. Is this real democracy? Is this real one-person, one-vote? Whether it is or is not ... this is how the Electoral College works.*

The intent of the framers was to devise a system that would, first and foremost, keep states committed to the idea of a collective union, secondly, they wanted a presidential selection system that could be supported by the people, and yet not become inherently subordinate to the other two branches. The selection of the president and vice president by electors who are chosen by the various states seemed to have been the ticket. But when originally transcribed, there was no intent to include the black or brown vote. Hence, there has always been efforts to exclude the black and brown vote — even by illegal means.

The two states that offer the most striking statistical example of the Electoral College's unfairness are Mississippi and Texas. The African American population in Mississippi currently hovers around 38%, while Hispanics comprise about 39% of the total population in Texas. Yet, the last time that both Mississippi and Texas cast their Electoral College votes for a Democratic candidate was in the 1960 election of John F. Kennedy when the white south was still voting Democratic (before the 1964 Civil Rights Act and the 1965 Voting Rights Act).

Because the WTA (winner take all) rule is followed by all but two of the states in the Electoral College, it is required that minorities **"First"** out-vote their white counterpart. That's a tall order because Mississippi has the highest population percentage of African Americans, and they're only at 38%; giving whites close to a 2-1 margin. Secondly, all the state's election offices are run and controlled by whites, and finally, almost all voter suppression tactics have the greatest impact on African Americans.

In Texas, Hispanics may comprise almost 40% of the population but only 30% of the eligible voters. Because Texas is a WTA state, Texas Hispanics have the same problem that blacks have in Mississippi — they have to first out-vote the majority in their state for their vote to count. And if they don't out-vote the majority, all of their votes go to the candidate that worked so hard to defeat. Your vote shouldn't go to the candidate you worked to keep out of office.

No other nation in the world, nor any state in the country has an Electoral College to select its leader after the people have exercised their choice. And in some cases, as it was in 1824, 1876, 1888, 2000 and 2016, the Electoral College chose someone other than the candidate favored by the people. It's tantamount to *"Elector Nullification"*. The primary purpose of a democratic form of government is to give those to be governed, the opportunity to choose those who would govern them. A system that would allow 270 people to decide who will govern 326,000,000, after the *majority* of those who were qualified to vote — and decided to vote (139,000,000) — chose a different candidate, can't really be called a democratic system.

On the Monday after the second Wednesday in December, (after voters have cast their votes for the President and Vice President on the Tuesday following the first Monday in the month of November) electors meet in their respective states and vote for the President and Vice President of the United States of America. States have the latitude to determine how electors will be selected for the Electoral College. The total number of electors is determined by the number of U.S. Representatives and Senators each state is allowed, which is determined by the census taken every ten years. In this census, all persons in the country are counted (citizens and non-citizens alike). So, Congresspersons represent *"All"* the people of this country ... not just the citizens of this country.

Article I of the constitution allows each state to have two U.S. Senators and an appropriate number of representatives based on the total population of the state *(no less than 1 representative and 2 senators per state)*. The 23rd Amendment gave the District of Columbia 3 Electoral College votes, as if the district were a stand-alone, individual state.

The reapportionment Act of 1929 set the number of U.S. House seats at 435, therefore, representation for the various states is determined by dividing the total population of the United States by the number of authorized voting members of the House of Representatives, i.e. 326,000,000 / 435 = X. The product in this equation (749,425) represents the total population required for each House District. By this calculation California is allowed 53 representatives and Wyoming is allowed only one. States may gain or lose representatives after each census. The total number of representatives is added to the total number of U.S. Senators (2) to determine the number of Electoral College votes each state is allowed. North Carolina with its 10 million residents is the ninth largest state in the country and is authorized 13 House Districts plus 2 U.S. Senators, giving it a total of 15 Electoral College votes.

All states (with the exception of Maine and Nebraska) have a *winner-take-all* system whereby they award all of its Electoral College votes to the candidate that wins the popular vote in that state. Maine and Nebraska have a proportional distribution system that awards a candidate a number of Electoral College votes commensurate with his share of the popular vote. This system of awarding all the Electoral College votes to the candidate who won the popular vote is tantamount to taking votes from one candidate and giving them to another. But if every state had a proportional distribution system, would there be a need for an Electoral College system? ... *my point exactly!* For many who oppose the Electoral College, this is the their greatest bone of contention. This is discussed in greater detail in chapter VI.

In his book *"Picking the President"*, Eric Burin has some compelling arguments regarding the initial intent of the Electoral College. Citing Hamilton in *Federalist 68,* he concludes that Hamilton felt that the Electoral College had two possible interpretations — (1) Insurance or (2) a representative body. Given the advantages of the internet, and other high-speed communications, an exacted nation-wide popular vote is possible today, so again ... what would be the need for an Electoral College system today? That brings us to the only sane reason for ever considering an Electoral College system. As we will remember, the percentage of the general populous that could read and write was very, very low in 1787. So, having an institution that would insure voters against themselves was not a bad idea. This is what was obviously on Burin's mind when the wrote: *"My personal feeling, by the way, is that insurance is the true purpose of the Electoral College".*

Burin clarity is unmistakable. He clearly questions the usefulness of the Electoral College today. I wholeheartedly concur with Mr. Burin's sentiments. Further, I believe it can be argued that the manner-in-which the states are geographically constructed greatly determines the outcome of presidential elections. Imagine for the moment that California were balkanized into 7 states instead of one. Each state, if equally divided, would have approximately 5.7 million residents *(10 times the population of Wyoming)*. Under this configuration, during a contentious election the House of Representatives would need 29 states to choose the president instead of the 26 required today. That's if we divide California and don't divide or combine any other states. Another pressing scenario would be the *combining* of southern or mountain states such as Idaho, Montana, Wyoming, Utah, North Dakota, and South Dakota. Presently these 6 states have a total of 22 Electoral College votes. If we combined them, they would have 11 Electoral College votes — clearly a 11-vote advantage in the current Electoral College and a 5-point edge in a contentious election.

Figure 1

Combining Mountain States

STATE	APPROXIMATE POPULATION	Current Individual ECV and CE Votes	Current Combined ECVs	Proposed Combined ECVs	Current Advantage
Utah	3,161,105	6	22	11	+11
Idaho	1,754,208	4	22	11	+11
Montana	1,062,305	3	22	11	+11
South Dakota	822,235	3	22	11	+11
North Dakota	760,077	3	22	11	+11
Wyoming	577,737	3	22	11	+11
Current Contentious Elections	As stated	1 each 6 total	N/A	N/A	N/A
Proposed Contentious Elections	8,137,667	1	N/A	1	- 5

Figure created by *"The Electoral College and the Black and Brown Vote"*

Figure 2

Separating California

STATE	APPROXIMATE POPULATION	Proposed ECVs or CE votes	Proposed E C V Districts or CE votes	Proposed Combined ECVs	Proposed Advantage
California	40,000,000	55	53	55	N/A
States 1-7	5, 714,285 each	9 each	7	63	+ 8
Current Contentious Elections	40,000,000	1	1	1	N/A
Proposed Contentious Elections	5,714,285 each	7	7	7	+6

Figure created by *"The Electoral College and the Black and Brown Vote"*

California is currently the most populous state in our nation, having over 40 million residents which allows her 53 Congressional Districts. Her two U.S. Senators give her a total of 55 Electoral College votes — most in the country. However, if there were to be a contentious election where there is no candidate reaching 270 Electoral College votes, by law, the U.S. House of Representatives will choose the President and the U.S. Senate will choose the Vice President. In such cases each state is allowed only one vote. So, California with her 40 million residents becomes equal to Wyoming with her ½ million residents. Even worse is the possibility of the House choosing a third-party candidate who received the least number of votes of the three highest receivers of votes cast. This means that if in 2020 Joe Biden would have receive 269 Electoral College votes, Donald Trump receive 268 Electoral College votes and David Duke receive 1 Electoral

College vote; the House of Representatives could **"*legally*"** make David Duke the next president of the United States of America. These are the rules of the game, and unfortunately most Americans know little if anything at all about the workings of the Electoral College that would allow a person receiving just 1 of the 538 votes cast to become president of the United States.

Most of us listen to news cast, read about the news on our devices, and some of us even talk to our friends and neighbors about our political system and who's lying and who's telling the truth. Then we watch CNN, MSNBC or FOX on the night of the election to get the updates and prognostications. The winner is declared by a major new network and we go away pleased, surprised, or sometimes even shocked. But what too many of us don't know is that the election is not decided that night, nor is it decided in the entire month of November. The election isn't decided until *"the Monday after the second Wednesday in December"*. And some would argue that even after the Electoral College votes to confirm the wishes of their particular state, the Congress could conceivably reverse that decision if when the Vice President presents the Electoral College results to the Congress, there are objections. If there are objections and one member from each house concurs in writing that they object, both houses will then go into conference to decide whether they should accept the presentation of the Electoral College or the objection of the members. A simple majority is required to overturn the Electoral College's vote. In the case of a very close election, the overturn of one state could swing the election for someone other than the individual decided upon by the Electoral College. In chapter 5 we discuss why the Electoral College hasn't changed over the years, and in chapter 7 we discuss some viable alternatives to this antiquated system. But for now, this is what we have. So, it would behoove us to learn how it works.

There are at least three issues with the Electoral College that need our attention immediately. First, there is concern about the House of Representatives making a highly political decision and rewarding an undeserving candidate the election.

First there is the aforementioned issue of selecting from the three candidates with the highest number of Electoral College votes.

Secondly, when there is a Contentious Election there are quorum requirements. The House of Representatives quorum requirement to resolve a Contentious Election is at least one member from two-thirds

(34) of the states must be present to convene a meeting. If, for instance, 18 states decided that because they have no chance to increase their numbers to 26 and award the election to their choice, they should refuse to attend the meeting — thereby eliminating the possibility of a quorum. Here again, we're hoping that the good folks in the House of Representatives will *"do the right thing"*. Thirdly, And lastly, the 12th Amendment states that if the House doesn't choose a President by March 4th, the Vice President becomes President. That is, of course, if there has been a Vice President chosen. In a Contentious Election in the Senate the 23rd Amendment gives the Senate 102 votes. Fifty-two senators are required to make a choice for the Vice Presidency. If the Senate splits their vote (51-51) the president of the senate (the siting Vice President) would cast the tie breaking vote which could be a vote for himself. It's not clear who becomes president until a president is chosen by the House or a Vice President is chosen by the Senate.

And this is partially how our Electoral College System works. There are tons of things that could be done better to improve the system, but until we make those changes it wouldn't hurt if we continued to participate in the electoral process *(continued to vote)* and learn as much as possible about the system, how it works, and what changes are needed. So, when someone calls, text, emails, or ask you about your view or opinion of the Electoral College, you'll have something better to say than … ***"huh?"***

And lastly, the first change to the 12th Amendment came after the election of 1800 when we saw that five was a very large number to choose from for the office of the presidency. We pared the number down from five to three. But there was obviously no consideration given to the possibility of having several candidates tied for third place. In this circumstance, do we consider all ties? Is there a method to select from those that are tied? ***There is not!*** We therefore label this as, *"unresolved issues and complications"*. We knowingly move forward with this imperfect system hoping that the time will not soon come when its imperfections are exposed for all to see.

The way the Electoral College system works as a political strategy is a bit more complicated. First of all, who are the winners and losers of the Electoral College system? The GOP is the beneficiary of the current construct of the Electoral College, but to fully understand why that is and exactly how it came to be, we must go back to 1965 and the passage of the 1965 Voting Rights Act. This act threatened the unfair electoral power of the south [although it didn't do anything to rein-in the contentious election inequities between states like California and Wyoming].

When the U.S. Constitution was established, Article I, Section II, Clause III afforded undo advantages to slaveholding states to secure their allegiance to the union. Slaveholding states were concerned that their small population would allow larger states to out-vote them in the House of Representatives and impact their Slavocracy. They therefore petitioned the framers to include a provision in the constitution to help them protect their slave economy and their way of life. Article I, Section II, Clause III states:

The basic meaning of the clause is that white free persons, white indentured servants and Indians that accepted their place and the rule of white men — who were not taxed —would be counted as whole persons. All others (meaning enslaved persons) would be counted as 3/5 of a person. This of course gave states with large numbers of slaves, a decided advantage in the House of Representatives. States like South Carolina and Mississippi whose slave population out-numbered their white population drew enormous advantages from Article I, Section II, Clause III. But little did most know that the 14th Amendment would give them even greater advantages. After the 14th Amendments were ratified, slaveholding states increased their unfair representation in the House of Representations by another 20%.

The reason slaveholding states were greatly advantaged has to do with voter suppression. The term voter suppression as defined today (curtail early voting, no same-day voting, voter I.D., moving precincts at the last minute, excessive vote file purges, assigning the worst voting machines to minority communities, and racial gerrymandering) would be euphemistic compared to the tactics of the Jim Crow era, when they would savagely beat voters, burn their homes, and businesses, or hang them by the neck for all to see. For almost 100 years, between the

15th Amendment (1870) and the 1965 Voting Rights Act, slaveholding states enjoyed counting their African American population to gain greater representation in the House of Representatives, and using voter suppression tactics to keep the vote relegated to white citizens only.

The 1965 Voting Rights Act with its preclearance clause made it more difficult for states with large minority populations to suppress their vote. The preclearance measure in Section 5 requires that before a state, or portions thereof, could make any changes to their voting procedures or requirements, they must be precleared by the Department of Justice or a three-judge panel in Washington. This protection of voting rights became the engine of the entire Voting Rights Act. There was a sunset provision included in the Act. The provisions of the act had to be re-authorized every 25 years. This became politically contentious at times, but all presidents would end-up signing the extension of the act, and it became normal theater.

In 1966, the first federal election after the passage of the 1965 Voting Rights Act, Republican operative Kevin Phillips was asked "What are we gonna do about all those niggers voting all over the south"? Phillips replied "Nothing, we'll do nothing. Let'um go, and when southern Democrats get tired of blacks invading their party we'll be here to welcome whites with open arms". Mr. Phillips couldn't have been more prophetic. Whites began to leave the Democratic Party in droves and re-registered as Republicans. Now the second step became easier … blacks we almost exclusively aligned with one party — the Democratic Party. This made it easier to use Gerrymandering against them, and easier to solidify the white vote.

Some say that the 1965 Voting Rights Act, nor the Shelby County v Holder decision have had little to no effect on the Electoral College, but I beg to differ. In North Carolina for instance, they both had everything to do with the Electoral College. The federal election immediately following Shelby v Holder, North Carolina's Congressional Delegation went from 8-7 Republican majority, to a 12-3 Republican majority. This is while Republicans comprise 30% of all registered voters in North Carolina but hold 80% of the Congressional Delegation. So, if there is a Contentious Election while there is an 80% Republican Delegation, for whom do you suppose the delegation would cast its lone vote for the presidency? And the likelihood of a Contentious Election is ever increasing with the hyper-polarization being exhibited between the two major parties, and the rise of credible third party candidates. It's no longer necessary to have the proverbial 269 tie for the presidential election to be thrown into the House of Representatives. If a Robert Byrd, Strom Thurmond, or George Wallace earns Electoral College votes when the candidates of the two major parties are running a very close race, we could have a Contentious Election without a 269-269 tie. If no candidates reaches 270, the House will choose the president … not just when there's a tie.

But even before the 270 question is answered, there is the determination of party strategies that impact the Electoral College regarding which states are visited and wooed, and which states are taken for granted and ignored. These strategies are born of party platforms and the planks that make-up their platform. These planks, this platform, nor the party strategy can stray too far from the overall party mantra that answers the questions … *"In what do we believe"? What do we value? and who are we?* The answer to these questions must be reflected in the party platform, or your party becomes conflicted and have a hard time selling itself to new voters as well as hanging-on to the older ones *(the base)*. So, when strategist look at the various states they first consider the state's voting history — its predilections. They then try to match specific states with a specific party based on predilections and mantras. In this match-up states begin falling to one side or the other. Those remaining are potential ***battleground states***. They are potential battleground states because we have yet to determine their value in *this* election. Their value in this election will be based on current *hot-button issues, and the favorite son phenomenon on both sides*. We then consider the prohibitive winnable and prohibitive losable states. What remains from that are the absolute ***Battleground states***. Strategies are developed based on funding, probability analysis and old fashion hip-pocket politics.

So now we have our battleground states that are gonna lead us to that magical number of **270**. We now journey down the path to convince the majority of the people in our battleground states why they should vote for our candidate. But we have to retreat to an earlier time to understand the next strategy. There was a time when strategist could be successful if they just make their candidate look good. Then we learned that making the other guy look bad was more effective than making our guy look good. We came up with ingenious ways to increase voter turnout in certain states and suppress the turnout in others. They started experimenting with *keeping the other guy's voter from showing up*. This was the beginning of voter suppression. Strategic voter suppression differed from voter intimidation in several ways. First and foremost was Strategic voter suppression's lack of violence. This approach made it more palatable to many conservatives that still considered themselves to be law abiding citizens.

The sophistication of demographic political software was the final tumbler to fall into place to ensure selective voter suppression. As the 4th U.S. Circuit Court said of North Carolina's Redistricting Plan ... *"They racially Gerrymandered its Congressional and State Legislative Districts with surgical precision"*. This ability afforded by the technological advances of software was enhanced by a decision by the high court ... "Rucho *v* Common Cause". In this decision, the court ruled that states may gerrymander is districts using hyper-partisan methods, and if citizens didn't like the gerrymandering they could vote the scoundrels out. My question was ... how do you vote a lawmaker out who has been given the authority to choose his own voters?

So, when we combine, Citizens United with Shelby *v* Holder, and Rucho *v* Common Cause, and when we allow *"Moscow Mitch"* and his sycophants to refuse to bring-up a bill to secure our elections from foreign interventions, we know that the going ain't gonna be easy. But nonetheless, elections will go on. So, we must be ready!

Contingent Elections: If no candidate receives at least 270 Electoral College votes, the U.S. House of Representatives will choose the President and the U.S. Senate will choose the Vice President. In Contingent Elections, each state will have only one vote *(this is where Wyoming becomes equal with California)*. My question has always been ... if all states become equal during a Contingent Election, why can't they be equal during regular elections? Or for that matter, why do states have to render their opinions after the citizens thereof have already spoken? We have the internet now, so we know the voting results of states instantaneously throughout the country. So, when the polls close from Maine to Florida and as far west as Texas, *(states that have a combined total of 416 Electoral College Votes)* California, Oregon, Washington, Alaska and Hawaii *(with their 122 collective ECV's)* have several hours before their polls close. And yet, the race could already have been decided while Californians are still waiting in line to vote. There are 416 Electoral College votes east of the Mountain Time Zone. A candidate only need 270 Electoral College votes to win. But none of this matters because the real vote won't be cast until the Monday after the second Wednesday in December; and it's possible that the presidency won't be decided even then *(if no candidates amasses 270 or more votes)*. If no candidate reaches 270 Electoral Votes, the House will choose the President, each state having just one vote. This means that 26 of the smallest states could get together and out vote the people of the most populous states. For example: The eleven most populous states have a total of 278 Electoral College votes *(or 52% of the total)*, but in a Contingent Elections they only make up 21.5% of the total votes in the Electoral College. So, the criteria becomes totally flipped on its head in a Contingent Election. In a regular elections we need 270 Electoral College Votes, but if no one reaches 270, the rules would allow the 26 least populous states, which have a total of 118 Electoral College votes to say who becomes president. And an added touch of spice is the measure of their choice. The 12th Amendment allows the U.S. House of Representatives to choose the president from the three top vote getters in the initial election for president. So, if candidate A receives 269 Electoral College votes, candidate B receives 268 Electoral College votes and a third candidate receives 1 Electoral College vote, the House could *(by law)* choose the candidate with 1 Electoral College vote. But in choosing from the three highest vote recipients the amendment doesn't mention or answer the questions regarding *"Ties for Third"*. It is highly probable that in such a case, the House would make their decision and allow one of the candidates that tied for third to bring the matter before the courts for resolution. Many constitutional scholars also think that the selection of a candidate with the least number of votes would avoid a prolonged conflagration between the two major parties.

Direct Law That Effect the Electoral College

12th Amendment: The 12th Amendment is the engine of the Electoral College. This amendment prescribes **how** the president is to be elected, and herein lies the rub. The framers were so anxious to wrap up the Constitutional Convention and get home that they were willing to do just about anything to bring closure to the process. The stumbling block seemed to have been the slaveholding states and smaller populated states' fear of being controlled by the large populated states. They therefore came up with a system (the Electoral College system) that would give a state like Wyoming as much power in choosing the president as a populous state like California — if there ever were a contentious election. But by-and-large the 12th Amendment was about making slave states feel that their ability to hold-on to their slaves, their economy, and their way of life would be protected.

20th Amendment: The 20th Amendment is primarily about the term of the president — when it starts and when it ends (Noon on January 20th after the election). Prior to the ratification of 20th Amendment, Presidents were installed in March.

22nd Amendment: The 22nd Amendment is sometimes referred to as the FDR (President Franklin Delano Roosevelt) amendment in that is prescribed the number of years or terms a President may serve.

23rd Amendment: The 23rd Amendment, ratified March 23, 1961, increased the number of electors from 535 to 538 and allowed citizen of the District of Columbia to vote for the President of the United States of America *(through their electors)*.

24th Amendment: This amendment eliminated yet another measure used by the south to suppress the vote of people of color. This amendment eliminated the poll tax. The poll tax was used to ensure that poor people (primarily black people) could not vote. In many cases it was retroactive, meaning that new voters had to pay poll taxes for all the years they didn't vote. This became a cumulative nightmare for people of color. Many poor whites were given poll tax waivers, or just weren't asked to pay. The amendment has taken on a modern hitch as states like North Carolina and Pennsylvania have required a type of voter I.D. that would cost voters a specific fee to qualify to vote. Proponents of the 24th Amendment have argued that the requirement of a special I.D. that turned-out to be a cost to the voter was in fact a *"Poll Tax"*. In the Supreme Court case *Crawford v Marion County Board of Elections,* the court held that an Indiana law that required voters to have a photographic I.D. was not unconstitutional. This is the cover that some states are using to require voters to produce an I.D. to vote. But states that require voters to have a specific I.D. could violate the 24th Amendment if that I.D. were costly or required a unusual cost in transportation or other cost measures to acquire the I.D.

26th Amendment: Opened the door to seeking younger voters to pre-register. The 26th Amendment grants voting privileges to 18 year old citizens. This voting amendment opened the door to the recruitment of potential voters as young as 16 years old to get involved in pre-registration.

McPherson *v* Blacker (1892): The court unanimously ruled that states may not be constrained regarding their determination of the apportionment of electors and their votes. This decision was reaffirmed by the court in its 2000 decision in Bush *v.* Gore.

Ray *v* Blair (1952): The court ruled that electors may not be compelled to pledge support to a particular candidate as a certification requirement to become an elector.

Citizens United *v* Federal Elections Commission (2010):

This ruling (more than any other) has changed our democracy, and not for the better. This ruling has had the effect of hanging a "for sale" sign on our elected officials and the laws they're responsible for creating, executing, and ruling on. Citizens United was the crowning achievement of those who choose to turn our democracy into a plutocracy and transforming our economic system (capitalism) into our religion.

Citizen United affects the Electoral College because it allows big money to threaten the candidacy of state legislators and congresspersons who support the replacement of the Electoral College system. Citizen United uses its dark money to get candidates running for the highest office in the land to kowtow to whomever has the biggest checkbook. It directly allows threats to incumbents to bend to the will of big money or see a multi-million dollar campaign contribution go to their opponents. What happened to "One Person – One Vote" and "Equal Protection Under the Law"?

Shelby Co. *v* **Holder (2013):**

This ruling effectively overturned the 1965 Voting Rights Act. Without Section 4(b) there is no coverage formula to determine which states or portions thereof are subject to Section 5 — which requires preclearance. And without preclearance considerable voter suppression damage can be done before the courts can rule that the action was unconstitutional. Further, any favorable court decision will not be retroactive; meaning that the affected election "Stands". The effect on the Electoral College is obvious. Gerrymandering Districts to gain control of the House of Representatives is just one example. Extreme Voter Suppression is another.

Without Sections 4(b) and 5 the 1965 Voting Rights Act is a toothless tiger with mush for claws. The court suggested that it was the responsibility of Congress to rewrite the language of the 1965 Voting Rights Act to comply with rulings of the court. Thus far Congress has not acted to rewrite Sections 4(b) and 5. And with a divided Congress and Republican president, there is little chance of that happening any time soon.

Rucho *v* **Common Cause (2019):**

This ruling practically gives permission to the party in power during redistricting to draw lines ensuring their reelection throughout the remainder of the decade … and well beyond. The solution offered by the court would have been comical if it weren't so serious. The court suggested that if voters were unhappy with the manner in which districts were drawn, they should vote the drawers of those districts out of office. My questions to the court is: "How do you vote someone out of office after the courts have given them the authority to choose their own voters?"

CHAPTER IV

Critical American Elections: 1800, 1824, 1876, 1888, 1968, 1980, 2000, 2008, 2012, 2016, 2020

To fully understand why the elections of 1800, 1824, 1876, 1888, and 1968 were specifically tied to slavery, reconstruction and subsequently to the black vote; we must first examine the politics of the slaveholding states.

At the turn of the 19th century, and during the presidential election of 1800, America had just been recognized by its former colonial boss (Great Briton - 1783) for just 17 years. In the next 19 years she will celebrate 200 years in the transatlantic slave-trade business, and she is still uneasy with the relationship between slave and slave-free states. Every political decision that slave states undertake have to go through the filter of the impact it'll have on slave states' ability to maintain and expand slavery. This is why the topic of slaveholding states is critically important to any political discussion in the era of legal slavery in America.

One of the slaveholding states' greatest fears was being out-voted in the House of Representatives by northern or slave-free states. Every measure was taken to avoid this circumstance, not the least of which was the 3/5 representation rule that allowed states to be given extra representation in the U.S. House of Representatives based on the number of slaves they owned. For every slave, states would receive 3/5 of a whole person added to the overall count to determine the number of U.S. Representatives allowed. One could readily see why slaveholding states supported this measure, but why would none slaveholding states support this as well? It could be the same reason that northern states did *absolutely nothing* when southern states appropriated United States forts, munitions, animals, and stores as they formally left the Union and joined the Confederate States of America. And, had Colonel Johnson surrendered when asked to do so by General Beauregard there might not have been a Civil War. *I may be working as an enslaved person instead of an author, but we wouldn't have had a civil war.* It also appears that from the beginning of the Republic, northern states have been about the business of trying to keep southern states from leaving the Union — *"Whatever it took; even the Electoral College".* There have been ten elections (1800 through 2016) and soon to be eleven, that have had a tremendous impact on our use of the Electoral College, and who we have become as Americans.

1800:

Thomas Jefferson   *John Adams*

In the United States Presidential election of 1800, sometimes referred to as the "Revolution of 1800," Vice President Thomas Jefferson defeated incumbent president John Adams.

In the last seven presidential election (1992 – 2016) Republicans have only won *one* popular vote election, and yet they won the presidency three times during the span of these seven elections. From 1992 through 2018 (26 years) Democrats have managed to get the majority of voters to side with them. But in some cases that's not enough. It's time for elections results to start reflecting the will of the people and become untethered to the 1700's. Should 21st century politics be contingent upon the whims of slavery bosses that existed more than 400 years ago? Slavery is dead, and so should be the Electoral College.

The United States is the only country (large or small) that has a ***"Three-Tiered"*** electoral system to elect their ranking leader. In Tier One the people vote (but their vote is the least consequential). There is no magic number to be reached to ensure victory by the popular vote. It is entirely possible (and legal) for a candidate to receive 100% of the popular vote and not be elected president. In Tier Two, the Electoral College Votes. Their vote is consequential if one candidate garners 270 or more Electoral College votes. However, "Faithless Electors" can override the Electoral College as does the Electoral College override the will of the people. Only 4 of the 51 participatory states appear to take "Faithless Electors" serious enough to enact punitive measures that discount the decisions of "Faithless Electors". But in the Third Tier the various states in the House of Representatives vote if there is no clear winner in Tier Two. In the Third Tier, each states gets one vote, making the 40 million people in California equal in voting strength with the ½ million in Wyoming. So … 26 states could bond together and elect whomever they choose as long as the candidate was one of the top 3 vote recipients in Tier Two.

1824:

In 1824, no one garnered the necessary Electoral College votes to outright win the Electoral College.

1824
■ **Andrew Jackson (D-R)** **Electoral** 99 **Popular** 153,544
■ **John Quincy Adams (D-R)** **Electoral** 84 **Popular** 108,740
■ **William H. Crawford (D-R)** **Electoral** 41 **Popular** 40,856
■ **Henry Clay (D-R)** **Electoral** 37 **Popular** 47,531

Jackson received the lion share of both the popular and the Electoral College vote (37.9% and 43.7% respectively). John Q. Adams (the eventual winner received the second highest vote in both categories (32.1% of the popular vote, and 31.0% of the Electoral College vote). So the decision (by law) was thrown into the U.S. House for resolution. The House voted for John Q. Adams … and the rest is history. The great question is *"Could this happen in the 21ˢᵗ century"*? The answer is a resounding **YES!**

That system, as archaic as it appears, still exist, and it may have become worse. Just suppose for the moment that this scenario replicates itself today, and this time the House can't come up with 26 states that agree on the same candidate … well, the Vice President (which is to be chosen by the U.S. Senate) becomes the President … unless there is tie vote in the senate. The question becomes … to whom does the presidency fall upon if the senate cannot come to a choice. We'll have to figure that one out when we get to it.

1876:

Rutherford B. Hayes   *Samuel J. Tilden*

1876
■ **Rutherford B. Hayes (R)** ✓   **Electoral** 185   **Popular** 4,036,298
■ **Samuel J. Tilden (D)**   **Electoral** 184   **Popular** 4,300,590

The 1876 United States presidential election was the 23rd quadrennial presidential election, held on Tuesday, November 7, 1876. It was one of the most contentious and controversial presidential elections in American history, and is known for being the catalyst for the end of Reconstruction. Republican nominee Rutherford B. Hayes faced Democrat Samuel J. Tilden. After a controversial post-election process, Hayes was declared the winner.

Many historians cite the 1876 presidential election as the beginning of Jim Crow and the end of Multiracial Democracy in America. The Freedmen's Bureau (under the auspices of The Reconstruction Act of 1867) set forth measures that led to the establishment of a majority black state legislature in South Carolina. Some say this was too much for white people to take. This was one of the key occurrences that led to Black Codes, Jim Crow, and the establishment and spread of white terrorist organizations like the Ku Klux Klan. Southern state conservatives (Democrats) like those in South Carolina and Mississippi knew they couldn't outright defeat the combination of black voters and radical Republicans. They knew that any outright violation of the law would be met with brute force. They therefore came up with ingenious statues, rulings, and methodologies to circumvent the laws that were established to promote and maintain **Democracy**. Among these statues, rulings and methodologies they supported to this end was ... the **Electoral College**. They could control voter suppression at the state level without too many problems, and Gerrymandering could help with Congressional representation. They could therefore focus their attention on the presidential elections, and the Electoral College seemed to be a very effective tool to help them continue their *"Way of life"*.

1888:

Benjamin Harrison   *Grover Cleveland*

The significance of the 1888 election was a repeat of the 1824 and 1876 elections in which the winner of the popular vote did not win the election. This was especially significant because the United States of America was seen around the world as *"An Experiment"*. It gave ammunition to the anti-democratic forces as they touted what they saw as the *misgivings of the Experiment*. First and foremost was the fact that only white male property owners could vote, secondly, slaves were counted as partial people for representative purposes. And finally, there was a concerted effort to suppress the vote of newly freed former enslaved people.

The election of 1888 was not very much unlike modern elections in that the most important issue of the day was not, race, race relations, voter access, or electoral law. The critical issue of the election of 1888 was *Free Trade vs Protectionism* — an economic issue. As it was then, so it is today ... Politicians are keenly aware that when given the options of the economy or electoral fairness, Americans will mostly choose the economy. This may answer the question why conservatives gravitate to economic issues over social issues, and why liberals generally focus on social issues. *Social Issues is where the people are, and Economic Issues is where the power is.* And, because we're a de jury democracy conservatives have to obfuscate the will of the people through Gerrymandering, Voter Suppression, and legal chicanery.

1888 Election Results

	Candidate	Party	Electoral Votes	Popular Votes
✓	Benjamin Harrison	Republican	233	5,439,853
	Grover Cleveland (I)	Democratic	168	5,540,309

This was the third presidential election that the collective people's choice was not honored. Instead, the second tier selected Benjamin Harrison who lost the popular vote to Grover Cleveland by over 100 thousand votes. Outsiders might ask ... how could a sitting president run for reelection and win by over 100,000 votes but lose the election — it's call the *Electoral College.*

1968:

Richard Nixon   *Hubert Humphrey*   *George Wallace*

In 1968 the critical issues were Civil Rights, The Vietnam War, and the Assassinations of Dr. Martin Luther King Jr. and Senator Robert Kennedy. There was a highly attractive third party candidate that ran under the American Independent Party label. Georgia Governor George Wallace ran as a third party candidate and received 46 Electoral College votes. And had Nixon's home state of California gone to Humphrey or Wallace, no candidate would have reached the required total of 270 electoral college votes. This would have thrown the election into the *"Third Tier"* and the U.S. House would have again (as they were in 1824) been required to select the president. In this process call *Contentious Elections,* each state, regardless of size, gets one vote. A candidate must receive votes from a least 26 states to claim victory in this selection process. Nixon having won 34 of the 51 states would have probable been selected by the House in a *Contentious Election.* However, electors have been known to become *"Faithless Electors" [electors who vote for a candidate other than their party candidate].* In 1968 Nixon won North Carolina; however one elector cast a vote for Wallace. Faithless Electors are handled differently by state.

In some states the penalty is cancelation of votes and replacement with an alternate Elector. In two states (North Carolina and Oklahoma) Faithless Electors may be charged with a civil violation (NC-$500.00, OK-$1,000.00). Their vote is cancelled and the Elector is replaced. In two other states (South Carolina and New Mexico) Faithless Electors may face criminal charges (SC-criminal conviction, NM-4th degree felony). Their votes are counted as cast.

The 1968 presidential race was about *"Race".* There were several lead-ups to the 1968 presidential election with its racial overtones. First, the Civil Rights Movement was in high gear in the '60's following the rambunctious '50's. In '64 the 1964 Civil Rights Act was enacted, and in '65 the crucial 1965 Voting Rights Act was signed into law. These two Acts caused considerable backlash from the anti-civil rights community.

The White Citizens Council and the Southern Manifesto are two anti-civil rights organizations that can be directly linked to the passage of the 64 and 65 Acts. Dr. Martin Luther King Jr. had become synonymous with civil rights, and Negro advancement. He was hated and targeted for this. His death shattered any semblance of peace and order in the black community. The urban riots that followed Dr. King's assassination in April of 1964 was used by conservative Republicans to gen-up rural and white anti-civil rights sentiments. Conservatives couldn't run an anti-civil rights campaign and expect to win … so they renamed it *"Law and Order"* and the *"War on Drugs"*. Who could be against law and order and the war on drugs? It was the beginning of sophisticated "Dog Whistles". Everybody knew what law and order really meant (arrest and lock-up street blacks, and arrest and kill drug users). These two initiatives did more to erase the gains made by the Civil Rights Movement than anything. Nixon saw where his operatives (Harry S. Dent Sr., Kevin Phillips, Lee Atwater, and Trent Lott) were and followed their lead. Their lead was … *"Show you are willing to stand up to the Negro and you'll get lots of white support"*. The 1968 Nixon campaign was the first modern openly racial election .. it wouldn't be the last. Nixon '68 was followed by Nixon '72. The country took a break and punished the GOP for Watergate in '76 by electing a peanut farmer from Georgia named Jimmy Carter.

1980:

Ronald Wilson Reagan　　　　　　*Jimmy Carter*

This election was a sea change election. The election of 1976 was in response to *"WATERGATE" and the resignation of Richard Nixon*. President Carter was not an awe inspiring leader. But he was just what the country needed to replace Richard Nixon & Spiro Agnew and Gerald Ford & Nelson Rockefeller. Ronald Reagan and George H.W. Bush had other ideas about the American electorate's desire and need to be the *"shinning city on top of the hill"*. They sold voters on the notion that Watergate was behind us, so we can get on with the business of the U.S. which is — ***Business!***

The critical unspoken factor in the presidential race of 1980 was *"Race"*. Ronald Reagan was the embodiment of racial dog whistles. He spoke clearly without uttering a word. The racially sensitive elements in the GOP knew what he meant, how it would be perceived by the rank and file white voter and how he should use his gift of acting to solidify his dog whistles and bumper-sticker slogans. Trent Lott (U.S. Senator from Mississippi, took Ronald Reagan to Neshoba County, Mississippi to kick-off his presidential campaign. Reagan was prepped by Lott to keep repeating the phrase **"States' Rights"**. They'll know exactly where you're coming from about so many things that really matter down here. That happened to be good advice from Senator Lott. Philadelphia, Mississippi is in Neshoba County where the three civil rights workers (Schwerner, Goodman and Chaney) were murdered in 1964. Whites all over the south that heard that speech instantly became Reagan supporters — even those that had never heard of California Governor Ronald Wilson Reagan before.

President Jimmy Carter was no match from the Actor from California — Ronald Wilson Reagan. Reagan was all that closet bigots and racist ever wanted. He brought the white male image to the forefront where it belonged, he conquered the known world by sitting-up the defeat of the Communist, he busted the unions, and led deinstitutionalization, increased homelessness exponentially, and made sure that people of color knew their places. This was the **_"REAL"_** American they had been looking for.

1992:

William J. Clinton　　　　　　*George H.W. Bush*　　　　　　*Ross Perot*

The GOP would probably have won the 1992 and 1996 presidential elections had the DNC not moved substantially to the right. After getting their heads handed to them over the three elections from 1980 through 1988 they decided they couldn't win with progressive and liberal ideals. They came up with something call the DLC (Democratic Leadership Council). This was a euphemism for let's leave the left and move more to the right to regain some of the suburban white voters who not only left the urban inner city, but left the Democratic Party as well. This effort was led by Al From, Bill Clinton, Al Gore, Chuck Robb, Bruce Babbitt, Lawton Chiles, Sam Nunn, Dick Gephardt, and Will Marshall. They were successful in convincing enough whites to return to the Democratic Party to win in 1992 and 1996 .

Ross Perot's role in the 1992 general election was impactful as well. Although Perot didn't garner any Electoral College votes, he did convince almost 20 million Americans to cast their vote for him, which turned out to be over 19% of the popular vote cast. But because of our winner take all Electoral College system Perot wasn't the majority vote recipient in any state and therefore his 20 million popular votes converted to exactly zero Electoral Votes. Any election system that would take the votes of 20 million people and give them to some candidate other than whom they were intended for needs to be changed.

Many feel that most of Perot supporters were Republicans that had drawn cold on President Bush. It is mathematically clear that had Perot's 20 million votes gone to President Bush, Bill Clinton would not have won.

2000:

George W. Bush   *Al Gore*

In the first presidential election of the 21st century we saw a tenacious group of GOP operatives refuse to be denied, while democrats were dressed in three piece suits with cases full of brief ready for any legal argument. But it wasn't a legal argument, it was a street fight. Who wins between a street fighter and a lawyer where there are no rules? Well, that's what happened in 2000 in Florida. George W. Bush became the 43 president of the United States of America.

When the Florida vote count was concluded by the Supreme Court, George Bush went on to become the 43 president of the United States of America. Bush won Florida by a mere 537 votes over Al Gore. And while Ralph Nader collected 97, 488 votes in Florida there were also approximately 19,000 young African American voters (many of them college students) that claimed they were disenfranchised. Out of the possible 116,488 voters could there have bee 538 that would have cast a vote for Gore? Many think so!

Even with the Supreme Court's ruling that made Bush the 43ʳᵈ president in the nation's history, Bush nonetheless failed to win the election where it counts — with the people! Vice President garnered 48.4 % of the popular vote compared to 47.9 percent for the *"winner"* George W. Bush. **The Electoral College Strikes Again!**

2008:

Barack Obama   *John McCain*

In the 2008 presidential election the entire election appeared to be about race. This was the first time in history that an African American was the nominee for president of a major political party in the United States of America. Barack H. Obama won the Democratic nomination and went on to become the 44ᵗʰ and only African American president of the United States of America.

Little did most Americans know that instead of America becoming *"Post Racial"* she would become mired more deeply in institutional racism. Many white voters who voted for Barack Obama in 2012 would find themselves casting a vote for a misogynist, a racist, a bigot, and a pathological liar.

2016:

Donald Trump   *Hillary Clinton*

Ironically Obama's two terms was the "firewood" for the emergence of a complete political novice named Donald J. Trump. The race based contingency in the country saw these two Obama elections as the last straw for the loss of their country, their culture and their complete way of life. This was it! They chose Trump over a field that contained 4 former GOP Governors, and 6 former and sitting GOP U.S. Senators.

Voters decided that they didn't need a curator to come in, and re-inventory and reorganize the china shop. They need a bull to come in and destroy the whole shop and start all over again. And that's what they got. Neither our friends nor our enemies recognize us anymore. They are wondering what happened to the US of A. With whom are they to invest their faith, who can they believe, who can they trust?

Little did most Americans know that instead of America becoming *"Post Racial"* she would become mired more deeply in institutional racism. Many white voters who voted for Barack Obama in 2012 would find themselves in 2016 casting a vote for a misogynist, a racist, a bigot, and a pathological liar. Let's see what happens in 2020.

2020:

Donald J. Trump   *Joe Biden*

The Electoral College voted on December 14, 2020. The results of their vote was: Joseph Biden, 306 votes and Donald Trump, 232 votes, projecting Joe Biden to become the 46th President Elect of the United States of America. President Elect Biden is scheduled to be sworn-in at noon, on January 20, 2021 by John Roberts, the Chief Justice of the United States Supreme Court.

This was a highly contentious race beginning with inaccurate polls, as was the case in 2016. The demographic exit polling of 2020 was surprising to say the least. The final tally of 306 to 232 also reflected a total popular vote victory of more than 6 million votes. The 74 Electoral College vote margin coupled with the 6 million popular vote margin means that Republicans have lost 7 of the last 8 presidential election popular votes. Could this have some baring on why they support the Electoral College and oppose any sort of popular vote system that would allow the people to directly choose the person that would govern them.

CHAPTER V

Why the Electoral College Continues ...

Despite Unresolved Issues, Complications and the Selection of 2nd Place Finishers

*Alexander Keyssar in his latest book **"Why do we still have the Electoral College?"** lays the question bare, and comprehensively attacks traditional rational for the continuation of this 18th century relic called the Electoral College. There are tons of reasons why we should discontinue the Electoral College, but only two reasons for its unchanged continuation — "small conservative leaning states and southern former Confederate states".*

*The WTA (Winner Take All), Two Party System, Hyper-partisanship, Outside Interference, Ties for Third, Faithless Electors, Contentious Elections, Election Quorums, March 4th Deadline, and the lack of parity between the popular vote and the electoral college vote... **ALL need resolutions, but somehow the Electoral College continues without fixes, despite these pressing needs.***

The U.S. Capitol Building, Washington, D.C.

Courtesy "Val Atkinson Photos"

Our Army was established in 1775, we declared our independence in 1776, and in 1783 the British Empire renounced any interest they may have had in that portion of North America now call *"The United States of America"*. Four years later, in 1787, we called our first Constitutional Convention to hammer-out the provisions of our newly found democracy. It would be helpful in trying to understand the intent and purpose of the framers and drafters of our constitution if we understand the loathing, the detestation, the abhorrence, the animus, and the out-right disgust they had for the way the British treated them *(the colonist)* during colonization. They wanted, above all, to ensure that they didn't have a form of government that in anyway resembled that of the British Empire. Above all they wanted a government of, for, and by, the PEOPLE! The first issue arose around the question of the type of government they would install. The idea of a representative government seemed to be well supported by most, but the question of what type of representative government came up when Virginia sought a Federal Legislature structured by the size *(population)* of each state, and New Jersey felt that each state ought to be represented equally. The Connecticut plan proved to be a reasonable compromise. The Connecticut plan *(introduced by Roger Sherman of Connecticut)* suggested that the lower chamber should be comprised of delegates from the various states and that each state's representation would be based on the total population of the state, whereas the upper house, or U.S. Senate, would have equal representation *(2 each)*. It was also decided that the federal government would be comprised of three co-equal branches of government — *The Legislature, The Executive, and the Judicial.*

Article I of the constitution established the *Legislative Branch,* or Congress. Article II established the *Executive Branch* of government. The chief executive officer was to be called the *President.* But things got sticky when the discussion turned to the method by which the president would be elected. There were those who wanted a president derived from the direct vote of the people — *The Popular Vote;* and some felt more comfortable with the *State Legislatures* making the choice, still others supported the idea that the choice should be left up to the *Congress.* Floating directly beneath the surface of these choices was the contentious issue of slavery and slaveholding states. Slaveholding states wanted the power to maintain their system over the objections of northern states that were not so economically dependent on the institution of slavery. Northern states wanted to preserve the Union, they therefore became amenable to concerns raised by slaveholding states that might eventually threaten the cohesiveness of the Union. This built-in crack in the dyke became a major source of contention as the American Experiment grew — culminating in the American Civil War in 1861. And, some say, it still hasn't been resolved today. It appears that we've decided to resolve the various unresolved issues as they reappear — ***hoping*** that they won't reappear too often. Some of the unresolved issues still with us are:

TIES FOR THIRD:

The 12th Amendment was ratified in 1803 to account for some obvious failings; one was the power of Congress to choose the president from the top five candidates. Five was too many candidates to deal with, so they reduced the number to three.

This means that *If on Monday, December 14, 2020 when the Electoral College votes to reelect the 45ᵗʰ president, or elect the 46ᵗʰ president of the United States, the Electoral College vote distribution is:*

Joe Biden — 238
Donald Trump — 200
Rand Paul — 50
Jill Stein — 50

two great problems would emerge. First of all, because no candidate would receive 270 Electoral College votes, the House of Representatives would *choose the president from the top **three** candidates,* and the Senate would *choose the Vice president from the top two candidates.* Secondly, in the example displayed above, Rand Paul and Jill Stein cannot both be considered for the presidency — only one, but which one?

FAITHLESS ELECTORS:

Faithless Electors are not bound to vote for the candidate of the party they represent, not even after Chiafalo *v.* Washington. If there is no collective remedy for this oversight, is the Electoral College an accurate representation of the people? Should the 12ᵗʰ Amendment be altered to require electors to vote as the people have voted, or should the vote distribution be proportional? In Chiafalo *v.* Washington the court ruled that Electors must vote as directed by their states. This may have been a victory for the state of Washington that required Chiafalo to pay the $1,000.00 fine assessed by the state of Washington for being a *"Faithless Elector"* in the 2016 general election for President of the United States, but it was also a victory for the NPVIC (National Popular Vote Interstate Compact). NPVIC opponents have long argued that it would be unconstitutional for Electors to vote against the will of a state's popular vote. Chiafalo clearly allows states to set rules that would mandate that all of their Electors vote for the candidate that won the *National Popular Vote.* This would ensure, of course, that the second or third place popular vote winner does not become president of the United States.

GIVERS AND TAKERS:

Another issue that needs to be considered when we look at the question of *"Why should the Electoral College Continue?"* is who are the givers and takers in the distribution of resources of the economy and national defense. All states that join the union are afforded the protection of the full forces of the United States of America regardless of their level of contributions to the nation's ability to provide for the economic security and military capabilities of all Americans. This means that the approximate 580,000 citizens in Wyoming that collectively contribute far less than the total citizenship of New York, Florida, Texas or California; are nonetheless entitled to the same protections as the citizens in those states that contribute far more in all categories to the federal government. At the same time, Wyoming, South Dakota, Delaware, nor Mississippi should be afforded special privileges because of their political settings. The case is clear that the old confederate states, combined with the mountain west states are the heart and soul of the Electoral College. And without them this relic called the Electoral College would implode for all the *right* reasons.

GERRYMANDERED CONGRESSIONAL DELEGATIONS

State Congressional Delegations are comprised of the number of Representatives of the various Districts within a state and the state's two U.S. Senators. North Carolina (for example) has thirteen Congressional Districts and two U.S. Senators giving her a total of fifteen members in her Congressional Delegation (also 15 Electoral College votes). Thirty percent of registered voters in North Carolina are Republicans and yet the GOP has eighty percent of the North Carolina Congressional Delegation (10 Representatives out of 13, and both U.S. Senators). The courts have stated that the *"Redistricting"* maps used to elect Congressional and State District Representatives was done with *"surgical precision"* to disadvantage Democrats and give advantages to Republicans. So… If there is a Contentious Election and the choice is thrown into the House of Representatives, Gerrymandering practically determines the presidency. Should this be changed? Would a national popular vote be helpful here?

THE THREE TIERED PROCESS

(Most Powerful = The Vote of the States, Least Powerful = The Vote of the People)

The *"Three Tiered Process"* will not be found while unearthing the nuances of America's election system called The Electoral College. This is an invention of mine that I thought would be apropos for the Electoral College. When the process is considered as a full process with separately functioning parts, it becomes easier to understand what each tier does, when, and why. More importantly, it exposes the weakness of the popular vote and why it needs to be strengthened. It also exposes the illogic of the reason for disallowing larger states to choose popular sons. And finally, it exposes how a very small minority of people and states can control the majority.

Today we have instantaneous news reports. Candidates are able to talk to the entire nation and each other simultaneously. The requirement that the president or the vice president must be from a state other than the elector practically eliminates the favorite son issue, and there seems no need to **NOT** federalize the election for President and Vice President. Such federalization would all but eliminate certain election chicanery that presently exist in practically every state in the Union.

Tier One ————— THE POPULAR VOTE takes place on the first Tuesday following the first Monday in November of the presidential election year (every four years). This is the vote that most Americans thinks decides the election, but it doesn't. The popular vote can be, and has been, overridden by the Electoral College … five times already, making the popular vote the least effective of the three tiers.

Tier Two ————— *THE ELECTORAL COLLEGE votes on the Monday following the second Wednesday in December of the presential election year. The Electoral College vote trumps the popular vote, the popular vote has no binding on the Electoral College vote. Electors are not bound to vote for the party they represent in the college. Although the vote of the Electors cannot be overruled by the popular vote, it is subject to reversal by the vote of the Congress. A candidate may receive a plurality of the votes (269 votes), but not a majority (270 votes). In this case the Congress may override the Electoral College. Tier One results may have chosen candidate A, Tier Two results may support Candidate B, but both Tiers One and Two may be overruled by Tier Three.*

Tier Three ————— *THE HOUSE OF REPRESENTATIVES votes if the Electoral College fails to come to a choice. The 12th Amendment states that if no candidate receives 270 or more Electoral College votes, the U.S. House of Representatives will allot one vote to each state. There will be a total of 51 countable votes. In order for a candidate to be selected by the House, the candidate must receive a majority of the 51 votes (26 states). The Third Tier is final. Neither of the first two Tiers can override the Third Tier. The Third Tier is therefore most powerful. It is most notable that in this tier, smaller states have equal power with larger states (one vote per state, regardless of size). It appears that the Electoral College is therefore more about states than it is about people.*

So why still have such a system that clearly favors slaveholding states 155 years after slavery has officially ended in the United States of America? Northern states aren't afraid that smaller states will again secede from the Union. They've counted the Electoral College votes and they know that the total number of Electoral College votes in the states of the old Confederacy *Tennessee, Arkansas, Texas, Louisiana, Mississippi, Alabama, Florida, Georgia, South Carolina, North Carolina and Virginia* total 160. And when we add the border states *(Missouri, Kentucky and West Virginia)* that generally vote with their conservative neighbors we have a total of 183 Electoral College votes. That's only 87 votes away from that magical number of 270. When we add in the mountain states that have recently been voting with the conservative states in the country *(Idaho, Montana, Wyoming, Utah, North Dakota,*

South Dakota, Nebraska, Kansas and Oklahoma) along with the newly acquired conservative states of *Iowa, Wisconsin, Indiana and Ohio,* we reach a total of 269 Electoral College vote. This effectively bypasses the tier one popular vote because it denies any other opponent the possibility of garnering 270 votes. In this vote count scenario the vote is guaranteed to go to the Congress because no candidate will receive 270 Electoral College votes. These states also add up to a total of 27 individual states — one more than needed to win the election in the third tier (U.S. House of Representatives). This may shed a little more light on why conservatives in general and Republicans in Particular want to keep the election away from the popular vote — where they don't do well at all. They've lost the popular vote in six of the last seven presidential races, and yet because of the Electoral College they've won three of those seven elections. They do well when the vote is decided by the Electoral College and they do very well if the vote is decided by the Congress.

Conservatives, the GOP and those that are afraid of the changing demographics in America will not allow a popular vote to determine the presidency of the United States of America — ***But they want us to believe that we're still the world's greatest DEMOCRACY!***

Despite all the flaws and incompletions, the Electoral College seems to keep chugging along. It still serves its purpose of keeping the small states and southern states happy, and recently it has added a new group of supporters. Let's call them *Patriots,* not in the sense that they're more patriotic than the rest of us, but because they *think* they are. They're the ones who see the Electoral College as an American institution that should be protected at all cost. And they fervently believe that if we lose this institution we're somehow losing a part of Americana. And that partly true; we would lose a part of Americana if we lost the Electoral College, but we'd be losing a part that needs to be lost. The Constitution, although brilliantly written, is not perfect. If it were, there would be no need to have an amendment process. The framers knew that the passing of time brings about change and they wanted our governing document to be flexible enough to withstand the strong winds of change and still be a governing document that we cherish.

But the most glaring reason that the Electoral College continues today despite the unresolved issues, complication and the selection of the election's *"Runner-Up"*, is the reliability of its racial control. There's no great danger of the south seceding from the Union again, but the GOP has staked its winning strategy on securing the backing and support of the solid south in every presidential elections since Richard Nixon's *"Southern Strategy"* election of 1968.

The GOP has moved so far to the right that it has to keep the solid south in tack or they have no chance of winning national elections. And with the defection of Florida, Virginia and North Carolina to Barack Obama the GOP literally became livid. They vowed to release the *"Jennie"* from the bottle even if chances were against them getting it back in. This meant Gerrymandering, Voter Suppression, false voter file purges, and by all means, it required the *retention of the Electoral College.* Without the Electoral College the GOP's national political election strategy would have to go through an extreme make-over. They'd have to appeal less to the white nationalist and more to people of color — all over America. And if a Democratic presidential candidate has long coattails and helps get some of his party's congressional candidates elected, the entire conservative paradigm would have to change. Even if the Electoral College remained in place and the National Popular Vote Interstate Compact became effective, things would change dramatically.

After Nixon's 1968 victory over Vice President Hubert Humphrey and Governor George Wallace, Senator Birch Bayh, Democrat from Indiana, and Representative Emanuel Celler, Democrat from New York, introduced a bill on September 8, 1970 that would have eliminated the Electoral College. Initially it even had backing from president Nixon himself. But the bill was filibustered to death and could not muster enough votes to bring about the 67 votes necessary to bring about cloture. Today it would be much more difficult to introduce a bill to eliminate the Electoral College. First, they'd have to introduce a bill that passes both houses of congress (290 votes in the House and 67 votes in the Senate) and then get 38 of the 50 states to vote for ratification. With today's hyper-polarized political environment the congressional two-thirds requirement and the states' three-fourths requirement could be reduced to a *"Majority"* requirement and it would still be very difficult to eliminate the Electoral College through the Amendment process.

Everything that may impact the Electoral College has become hyper-political. Therefore, the Electoral College continues because our elected officials can't muster the fortitude to do what's right and *"Let the People Pick the President"*. In the following chapter (under Remedies) alternatives to the Electoral College without pursuing the amendment process are discussed.

CHAPTER VI

The Electoral College and The Black and Brown Vote

The Washington Monument, Washington, D.C.

Courtesy "Val Atkinson Photos"

*B*lack and Brown votes have always been problematic for white folks in America. The very mention of the phrase 'Black & Brown Vote' fosters feelings of fear and anxiety among too many whites.

Often, there are white fringe groups that see non-whites as a threat to the natural order of things, like white supremacy and the resulting white privilege. And many of those whites who fought and died for the right to kill, rule-over, and own black people are now being lauded for their failed *attempt at instituting a Slaveocracy that would have run from Anchorage to Argentina had they been successful in the Civil War. And it appears that the Electoral College as presently administered, may have rescued the former Confederacy from total political defeat.*

It's one thing to have your vote not cast for the person you're supporting, but to give that vote to the person you're actually going to the polls to vote against is not only undemocratic, it's cruel and borders on the criminal. The Electoral College is the most anti-democratic system allowed to exist in the so-called Free World.

The first order of business in understanding why the Electoral College is not good for America (and especially unfair to Black and Brown voters) is to understand why and how the Electoral College came about in 1787, secondly, it's important to understand what impact it's still having today. And we must understand where things stand demographically in America today, and how the votes are **REALLY** counted. So let's start with the demographics.

DEMOGRAPHICS:

Taking the last item first, it's estimated by some demographers that by 2042 the white population in the U.S. will be less than 50% of the total population — making this a *"Majority – Minority country in white or European terms"*. The very thought of this idea is scary for too many white people in America. *But before we continue, let's unpack this statement and it relative meaning. Just what is a 'majority-minority' country? In the broader sense, a majority-minority country is one in which the majority of the country is made-up of minorities. Well, just what or who are minorities? Minorities are peoples who cannot be classified as a member of the majority race or ethnic group. In the case of the United States of America, minorities are people who are not white. This differs from the world definition of minority. In the world population, white people are actually the minority, making up about 11 percent of the world's population. So, when people are referred to as minorities here in America, they're talking about the non-white demographic makeup of the United*

States. Globally, Asians and people from the sub-continent of India makeup over 40% of the world's population, and some demographers anticipate that that number could rise to 50% by mid-century. The United States of America (on the other hand) with its 327 millions residents, comprise about 4.8% of the world's population.

So, if demographers are correct, blacks and browns, yellows and reds will constitute the majority of Americans by the year 2042. White America will have to build coalitions with peoples of color to maintain their political dominance. This may not be a bad idea, if it works like the parliamentary procedures in Europe.

America's Brown Vote: *Now, and in the Future*

Figure 7

In the 2020 presidential election, the Hispanic Battleground States vote totaled as follows:

State	Biden	Trump	% of Total
PA	78%	18%	4%
GA	57%	41%	5%
AR	63%	33%	19%
NV	56%	37%	19%
CO	60%	35%	11%
MI	*Biden captured 59% of the Hispanic vote in 2020 as did Clinton in 2016 Trump did better in 2016 than in 2020 by 1%*		
WI	*Biden captured 60% of the Hispanic vote in 2020, Clinton 63% in 2016 Trump did worse in 2020 than in 2016 by 1%*		
NC	59%	39%	5%
FL	52%	47%	19%
TX	59%	40%	19%

The significance of this chart is the fact that in no battleground state did Trump win the Hispanic vote — not even in the battleground states he won (North Carolina, Florida and Texas).

Demographers predict that in the foreseeable future, the largest minority population in the country will continue to be Hispanics. This means that if the GOP has any plans to take back the popular vote from the Democrats it must include getting a much larger share of the Hispanic vote — particularly the young Hispanic vote. Some of the exit polling from the 2020 general election does not bode well for this challenge.

The polls indicate that 65% of all Hispanics voted for Biden and only 32% for Trump. Almost 70% of young Hispanics (18-29) voted for Biden, and there was no age group that gave Trump the majority of their vote. This is very problematic for the GOP. This means that the GOP is faced with the dilemma of staying the course and perpetually losing the popular vote, or enlarging their tent to attract more Hispanics and African Americans, which will almost assuredly cause losses in their interior base of the deep south and the mountain west. It also looks like it's *"choose your poison"* time for the Republican Party.

Listed below are demographic results of exit polling that give reason to Joe Biden's and Kamala Harris' decisive victory in the 2020 presidential election.

Figure 8

Democrat percentages on first line, Republican percentages on second line

Gender

Male (48%)

45%

53%

Female (52%)

57%

42%

Race

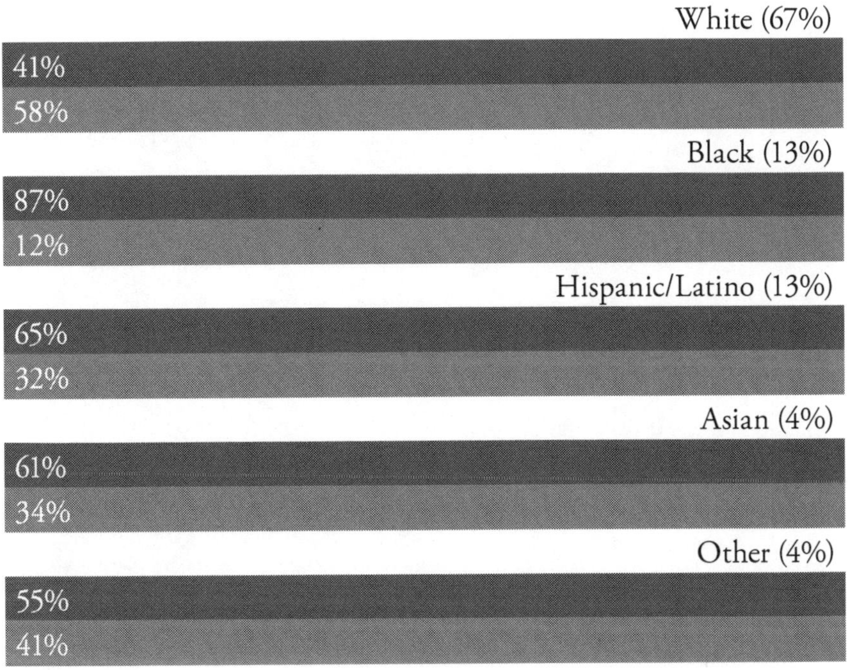

White (67%)

41%

58%

Black (13%)

87%

12%

Hispanic/Latino (13%)

65%

32%

Asian (4%)

61%

34%

Other (4%)

55%

41%

Race

White (67%)

41%

58%

Non-White (33%)

71%

26%

Sex by race

White men (35%)

38%

61%

White women (32%)

44%

55%

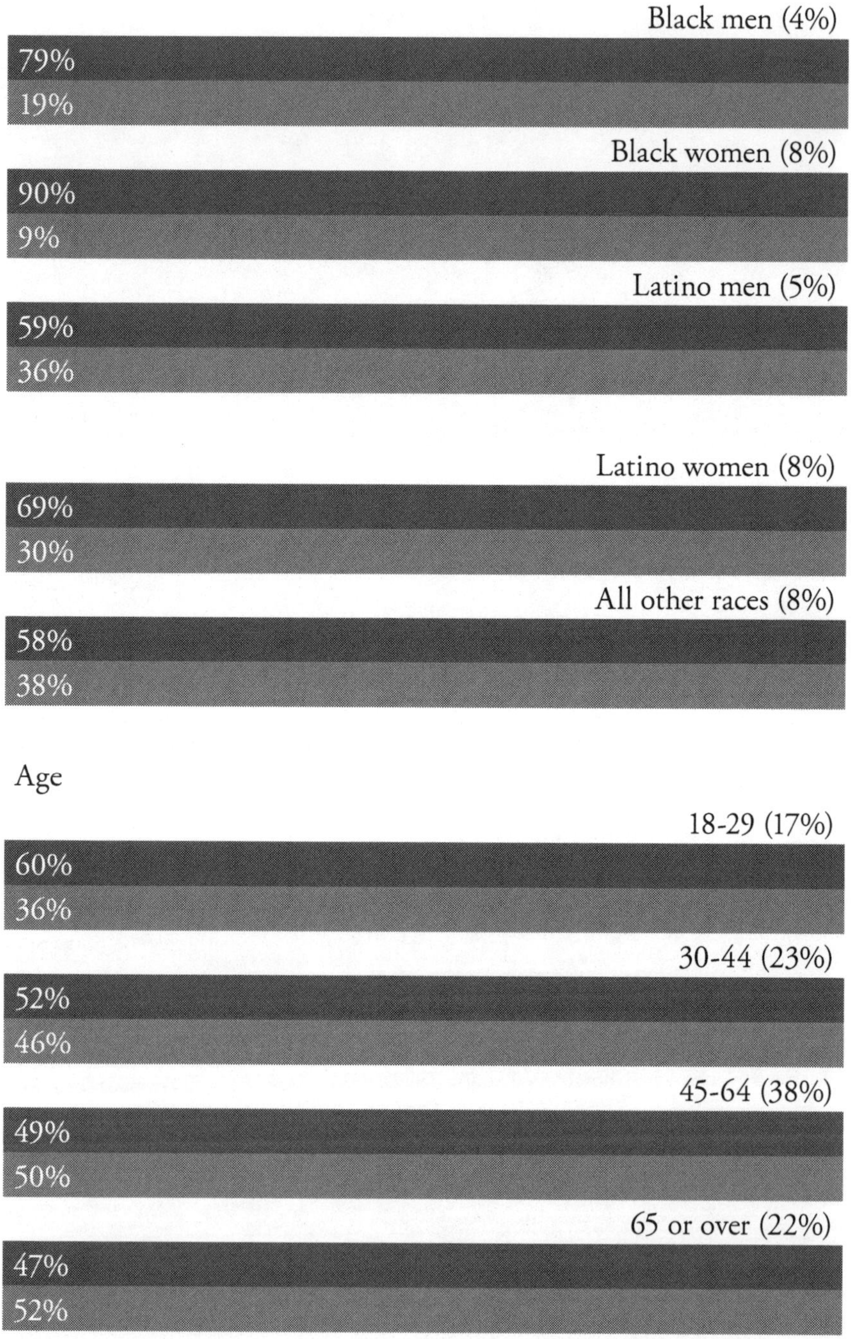

Black men (4%)

79%

19%

Black women (8%)

90%

9%

Latino men (5%)

59%

36%

Latino women (8%)

69%

30%

All other races (8%)

58%

38%

Age

18-29 (17%)

60%

36%

30-44 (23%)

52%

46%

45-64 (38%)

49%

50%

65 or over (22%)

47%

52%

Age

18-44 (40%)

56%

42%

45+ (60%)

48%

51%

Age

18-24 (9%)

65%

31%

25-29 (7%)

54%

43%

30-39 (16%)

51%

46%

40-49 (16%)

54%

44%

50-64 (30%)

47%

52%

65 or over (22%)

47%

52%

Age by race

White 18-29 (8%)

44%

53%

White 30-44 (14%)

41%

57%

White 45-59 (19%)

38%

61%

White 60+ (26%)

42%

57%

Black 18-29 (3%)

89%

10%

Black 30-44 (4%)

78%

19%

Black 45-59 (3%)

89%

10%

Black 60+ (3%)

92%

7%

Latino 18-29 (4%)

69%

28%

Latino 30-44 (4%)

62%

34%

Latino 45-59 (3%)

68%

30%

Latino 60+ (2%)

58%	
40%	

All other (8%)

57%	
38%	

Which best describes your education? You have:

Never attended college (19%)

46%	
54%	

Attended college but received no degree (23%)

51%	
47%	

Associate's degree (AA or AS) (16%)

47%	
50%	

Bachelor's degree (BA or BS) (27%)

51%	
47%	

An advanced degree after a bachelor's degree
(such as JD, MA, MBA, MD, PhD)(15%)

62%	
37%	

Poll results courtesy Albright Legend

Brown people that hail from south of America's border have been called many different names over the past 172 years *(since the end of the Mexican American War in 1848)*. They've been called *Mexicans, Hispanics, Latino & Latina,* and most recently they've been called *LatinX.* But only 3% of Brown people use the term *LatinX,* so herein I'll refer to my Brown brethren as *Hispanic.*

In 1803 the United States purchased **The Louisiana Purchase** from the French government which doubled the size of the United States. In the early 1840's the United States became interested in some of Mexico's most northern and western territories. If these territories could be purchased from Mexico, the United States of America would literally stretch from *sea to shining sea*. Of course, Mexico refuse to sell the land to the United States. But the U. S. wouldn't take no for an answer, and talk eventually led to war — the *Mexican American War* lasted from 1846 to 1848. The U.S. defeated Mexico in 1848 and usurped all or portions of what has become the states of California, Nevada, Utah, Wyoming, Arizona, New Mexico, Colorado, Kansas, Oklahoma, and Texas. The present-day Hispanic population in these states is very high due to the historical presence and linage of the Hispanic population. In 2020 the states with the highest percentage of Hispanic eligible voters are: *New Mexico – 42.8, California – 30.5, Texas – 30.4, Arizona – 23.6, Nevada – 19.7, Colorado – 15.9, Utah – 9.0, Wyoming – 7.4, Kansas – 7.1, and Oklahoma – 6.2.* Of these 10 states, Texas and Arizona *(both red states)* are considered to be very much in-play for the November 3, 2020 election.

In recent presidential elections the collective Hispanic vote was seen by many in the Democratic Party (as they saw the military vote) — **A Republican Lock!** This was especially true after the failed Bay of Pigs Invasion in 1961. During the Nixon administration, efforts were ramped-up to increase immigration from Cuba by anti-Castro Hispanics. They mostly migrated to Florida and became a highly dependable voting bloc for conservative Republicans. It wasn't until recently (the Obama administration) that Hispanics began to reconsider their allegiance to the GOP.

Fast forward to 2016 and we find that Hispanics are being trashed by the GOP nominee (Donald Trump). The GOP has a new strategy, and it appeals to whites who think that they've lost control of their borders and their culture. In 2016 Trump ran a campaign that appeals to the racism in white America. And sadly, he's doing the same thing in 2020. But through it all, thank goodness, Hispanics have seen the light and fled the GOP like it had the plague. Trump's embrace of white nationalism is gonna make it very difficult for him to regain the Black & Brown vote in 2020, but he's so locked-in and committed to the doctrine of *"White Privilege"* that if he tries to reconcile with Black and Brown Americans he'll undoubtable lose his core of white privileged voters. He's in what we call the proverbial *"Pickle.*

The 2020 battleground states are made up of the three states that gave Trump his narrow Electoral College win in 2016, *Wisconsin, Michigan and Pennsylvania*, plus North Carolina, Arizona and Florida. Making their way into the category of battleground states for the first time are *Georgia and Texas*. Wisconsin, Michigan, Pennsylvania Georgia and North Carolina don't have the Hispanic population impact that Arizona and Florida have but they're nonetheless very much in play for the Hispanic community. Arizona, Texas and Florida on the other hand are very heavily populated by Hispanic residents. And Florida, with its 29 Electoral College votes, has been the prize jewel in every election since the 2000 election when the Supreme Court ended-up selecting the 43rd president of the United States. Texas has the second largest Hispanic percentage of state population in the nation at 28.1%. Arizona is 4th with a percentage of 21.5%, followed by Florida at 18.5%. Texas has a very large Hispanic population but her African American population is comparatively small and the white population is very large, therefore Florida's Hispanic vote is more *impactful* that the Texas Hispanic vote.

The percentage of Hispanics who participate in political activities varies, but rarely exceeds half of those eligible. In general, Hispanics participate in common civic activities, such as voting, at a much lower rate than non-Hispanic Whites or Blacks. In the 2004 election 57.9 percent of the Hispanic VEP (voting eligible population) was registered to vote and 47.2 percent actually turned out to vote. The registration and turnout rates are approximately 10 percent lower than those of non-Hispanic blacks and 18 percent lower than those of non-Hispanic whites.

Puerto Rico citizen are American citizen and are allow to vote in Presidential elections if they meet the residency requirements of the state they choose to vote in. If in 2020, for example, thousands of Puerto Ricans decide to move to Florida, Georgia, Texas or North Carolina, and met all the requirements to register to vote 30 days before their voting date, they could have an impact on that state's election. This is not likely to happen however, due to the logistical and capital requirements that would be necessary to pull things together. The Trump Administration's response to Hurricane Maria didn't sit well with many Hispanics in the 50 states and Washington, D.C. This combined with the slanderous manner in which Donald Trump referred to Hispanics and other non – whites was enough to garner unsolicited support for former Vice President Joseph Biden.

Hispanics have become the largest minority in the country, out numbering the previous number one minority — African Americans. But these two minorities combined with other non-white Americans are expected to become the new majority in America over the next 15 – 20 years. This means that whites in and of themselves will no longer be able to control everything that happens politically in their country. This scares the *Bejesus* out of many white Americans. This, many say, accounts for the 62 million votes he received in 2016, and the 53% of the white female vote he garnered while being accused of sexual harassment and sexual assault in the campaign running up to the election. Additionally, his opponent was a female who had served as a former First Lady, Secretary of State, and U.S. Senator, and if elected she was to go on to become the first female to hold the highest office in the land. With his record of sexual harassment, sexual assault, and taking positions against a woman's right to choose; how Donald J. Trump still got 53% of white women to vote for him and against a highly qualified white woman to become the first female president of the United States of America is **ASTONISHING !**

The Hispanic vote, like the African American vote is subject to the loops and turns of an Electoral College ill-fitted for 21st century America. Hispanic voters in Texas and Florida shouldn't be required to out-vote their white counterparts in their state to have their votes cast for the candidate of their choice. As previously stated about African Americans in North Carolina — Hispanics in Texas make up about 28% of the population, but they need to out-vote the other 72% to have their vote cast for the candidate they desire. Just like African Americans, Hispanics aren't asking for the system to give them anything, but they are demanding that the system not take anything away either. And that's exactly what the current Electoral College system does ... it takes votes from one candidate and gives it to another in the *Unit System,* or *Winner Take All System.* This is not democratic and it shouldn't be happening in the United States of America.

The Hispanic Electorate in Florida

About 1.5 million Hispanics are eligible to vote in Florida, representing approximately 14 percent of the more than 11 million eligible voters in the state, according to a Pew Hispanic Center analysis of data from current population surveys conducted by the U.S. Bureau of the Census in 2003. Of those Florida Hispanics, who are U.S. citizens and at least 18 years old, some 540,000 or 36 percent identify themselves as being of Cuban origins, and another 480,000 or 32 percent identify as being of Puerto Rican origins. Another 315,000 or 21 percent trace their origins to Central and South America.

About 60 percent of Florida's Hispanic voters live in just three counties each with different characteristics.

Miami-Dade County is home to 590,000 Hispanic eligible voters or 39 percent of the state's Latino electorate, by far the largest concentration in the state. Two-thirds of them are of Cuban origins. Latinos account for 52 percent of the eligible voters in the county.

Orange County, where Orlando is located, is next largest with a Hispanic voting population of 166,000 or 11 percent of the state's Latino electorate. Two-thirds are of Puerto Rican origins. Latinos account for 14 percent of the county's voters.

Broward County, where Fort Lauderdale is located, has 165,000 Hispanic eligible voters or 11 percent of the state's Hispanic electorate. Central and South Americans are the largest Hispanic group in Broward, representing 42 percent of the county's Hispanic voters. Puerto Ricans are the next largest group with 30 percent and Cubans make up 20 percent of the Hispanic voters in Broward. Hispanics represent 14 percent of the county's voters.

The major Hispanic origin groups are distributed across Florida in distinctive geographic patterns:

Nearly three-quarters (73%) of Florida's Cuban voters live in Miami-Dade. The rest of the Cuban electorate is scattered across the state.

Puerto Rican voters are much more evenly distributed around the state. The largest concentration in any one county is the 23 percent of Puerto Rican voters in Orange County. Elsewhere, Miami-Dade (11%), Broward (10%) and Osceola (9%) also have significant shares of Florida's Puerto Rican voters.

The largest concentration of Central and South American voters is in Miami- Dade (38%). Other significant shares are located in Broward (22%) and Orange (11%).

Hispanics appeared to be in the center of the bull's eye in the election of 2020. This time it was due to Trump's new topnotch strategy to invalidate the election. His plan was based on the hope that the final Electoral College count would be within the total count of a very close race in a state that has more Electoral College votes than the margin that Joe Biden won by. An example would be if Biden won by less than 29 elector votes and won Florida in a very close race, then Trump would claim voter fraud in the state of Florida, ask for a recount, try to eliminate voters from certain counties or precincts that voted overwhelmingly for Joe Biden. If he could change just one state in this manner, he would change the election and claim he won by reversing voter fraud. So, his operatives will be scouring the election results very carefully to identify the state or states to charge with *"voter fraud"*. It's gotta be in the *"Goldie Lock Zone"*. It can't be a state with less than the number of electoral college votes that Biden won by, it can't be a state that won't give Trump enough electoral college votes to win even if **HIS** supreme court rules the state to be counted in his favor. And of course, it can't be a state that he won; **because we all know that there would be no voter fraud in states that he won,** just those states that Joe Biden and Kamala Harris won.

America's Black Vote: *Past, Present, and Future*

Status of Blacks and Browns when THE ELECTORAL COLLEGE WAS ESTABLISHED

In 1787, when the Electoral College was established, Blacks and Browns were ubiquitous but white supremacy was the unwritten and written law of the land. All that bothered to inquire knew that any mention of equality, fairness, justice, and freedom in the United States Constitution referred to the relationship between the former colonist and their former rulers — The British. Blacks and Browns were not citizens of the United States of America when the constitution was written. And in the Dred Scott decision the court ruled that Blacks were not and could not be citizens of the United States of America. Blacks were an enslaved people and Browns had their own country. The Native American question had yet to be settled. So, any mention of non-whites was from a property or territorial perspective.

In Article I, Section 2, Clause 3, it is very clearly laid out that white men are at the top of the political food chain, and all the rest was expected to remain in their places. This was the American Caste System in place in the 18th century (that actually began in the 15th century). In her book *"Caste: The Origin of our Discontents,* Isabel Wilkerson lays out prima facie evidence that America has played host to the longest running Caste System in the known world. She examines the system from the perspective of race and from a comparative angle with the Caste systems of the subcontinent of India and Nazi Germany's Third Reich. The oblique identification of black people in Article I of the Constitution [*"and 3/5 of all others"*] is indicative of the "Dalits, Untouchable, Bottom Rung status assigned to Africans in the Caste System of America's Antebellum era.

In this section of the Constitution, representation in the House of Representatives was to be determined by the whole number of citizens, not counting Indians not taxed, and 3/5 of all others. So, the actual count of Blacks was used to help bolster representation in the House of Representatives for slaveholders and thereby extra votes in the Electoral

College. So blacks played a role in determining the direction and flow of the country's election system … without doing a thing.

The presence of blacks would further help slaveholders and former slaveholders during and even after the Civil War. During the Civil War General Robert E. Lee wanted to allow the enlistment of enslaved Africans to fight for the Confederacy but Confederate President Jefferson Davis thought it was a bad idea. Davis was concerned that if the Confederate States of America was successful and defeated the United States of America, it could be difficult to recoup the weapons from the black soldiers; and more importantly, it would destroy the notion of black inferiority in the minds of blacks and whites alike. Jefferson Davis did however allow enslaved Africans to be used as non-combat aides and body servants. This arrangement freed thousands of Confederate soldiers to serve in direct combat roles that would have otherwise been used for non-combat support services such as cooks, wranglers, teamsters, and construction workers. After Reconstruction (and due to the ratification of the 14th Amendment) the states of the former Confederacy received a 20% bump in legislative representation over what they had in the antebellum days of the 3/5 rule.

During the Constitutional Convention of 1787 the framers were having issues with the completion of the second Article of the Constitution (The Executive Branch) but the status of non-white people was not one of those issues. Native Americans (red people) were the enemy, African Americans (black people) were slaves, and the brown people to the south were in possession of land that they didn't deserve, and would eventually become a part of the United States of America. So … without directly saying so, the Constitution was written by and for white people. This was the first known governing document that had such a strong inference of racism. It could be said that *"racism was 'baked-in' the Constitution"*.

One of the problems that the framers had was designing a governing document that would promote a sense of pride of ownership. So … historians had to be careful how they described critical historical facts. Red people (for example) were depicted by many as generous, cooperative partners in the transfer of land from Native Americans to the conquering

Europeans. Browns were depicted as tolerable, as long as they knew their places and stayed in them. But, blacks were a different issue. Whites that were being sold on the idea of ownership of other human beings, had to be convinced that the property label that was sought for the enslaved blacks was appropriate because they were actually *"sub-human"*. It became critically important to the survival of the institution of slavery that black people were seen as sub-humans. Once it became a part of the standing culture of settling Europeans that blacks were considered to be sub-human, it didn't matter whether you were a slaveholder or not, you were expected to approach the black question through the lens of his in-humanity. After this was established and reinforced, the culture of slavery and the following Jim Crow, discrimination, and out-right racism became an integral part of American culture. Even today we have whites who claim that the Civil War wasn't about slavery, but about the preservation of a way of life. This is so bazar. It's like saying *"using a shotgun to decapitate someone isn't killing, it's about controlling the population"*.

When the Electoral College was established, whites weren't concerned about the red, brown, or black population as much as they were about keeping the states together. The framers didn't want to give smaller or slaveholding states any reason to think that they wouldn't be able to protect their interest by joining a Union that was comprised of mainly non-slaveholding states. Thus, blacks became a critical entity within construction of American constitutional positions.

First, slaveholding states wanted their slaves to be counted when appropriations were being considered, but northern non-slaveholding states weren't about to allow the states of Mississippi and South Carolina *(which both had populations of slaves that outnumbered their white populations)* to become over-represented in the House of Representatives. Northern states knew that this overrepresentation would lead to long-standing committee chairmen that would be almost impossible to replace. Many felt that southern slaveholding states were being over-compensated for their populations. So ... the notion of counting slaves as three-fifths of a person for appropriation purposes was floated, then the bean-counters got involved and decided to increase the level of taxation leveed on states receiving additional Congressional seats. This led to slaveholding states feeling that they were paying for their overrepresentation, and therefore deserved it. Neither was true. Finally the 14th and 15th Amendments put to rest, once and for all, the question of *one person, one vote … except for the* **Electoral College**. The Electoral College makes some votes more valuable than others. The Wyoming — California paradigm comes to mind, where Wyoming's 260,000 voters have as much to say about who gets to be president as does California's almost 16,000,000 voters.

Article I, Section 2, Clause 3 of the U.S. Constitution states:

"Representatives and direct Taxes shall be apportioned among the several States which may be included within this Union, according to their respective Numbers, which shall be determined by adding to the whole Number of free Persons, including those bound to Service for a Term of Years, and excluding Indians not taxed, three fifths of all other Persons. The actual Enumeration shall be made within three Years after the first Meeting of the Congress of the United States, and within every subsequent Term of ten Years, in such Manner as they shall by Law direct. The Number of Representatives shall not exceed one for every thirty Thousand, but each State shall have at Least one Representative; and until such enumeration shall be made, the State of New Hampshire shall be entitled to chuse three, Massachusetts eight, Rhode-Island and Providence Plantations one, Connecticut five, New-York six, New Jersey four, Pennsylvania eight, Delaware one, Maryland six, Virginia ten, North Carolina five, South Carolina five, and Georgia three".

Without actually saying so, or using the words, the framers communicated to us their position on people of color — particularly black people *(three fifths of all other Persons)*. Since 1441, 1492 and 1619 marked the suffering of people of color at the hands of greedy Europeans, but the framers' made white supremacy an integral part of the American experiment in Article I, Section 2, Clause 3 of the U.S. Constitution.

How This Race "Mess" Got Started

1441

In 1441 a group of Portuguese sailors captured several Africans and returned them to Portugal to perform free labor. This was the beginning of Europe's involvement in the racist, white supremacy business of slave trading. During this era, The British Empire was the greatest beneficiary of the slave trade. They owned the colonies that enslaved Africans, who picked the cotton, cropped the tobacco, and harvested the sugar cane. The colonist managed the labor that made the money that the British used to finance its wars and continued world domination. And it was based on race. White people were seen as the slave masters while black people were seen as slaves. Some say it's still that way today.

1492

Christopher Columbus

After getting lost and landing in the Bahamas, Christopher Columbus and other Europeans quickly learned that the indigenous people of the Americas didn't have the means to defend themselves against European aggression. They began violating a central theme of Native American culture — *"Taking without asking".*

What has become known as *"Indigenous Peoples' Day"* was previously celebrated as Columbus Day. Celebrating October 14th as the day Europeans invaded the Americas and expecting Native Americans to participate in that celebration was asking a bit much. Nonetheless, this became the starting point for white supremacy in the Americas.

The indigenous people of the Americas have become to be known as Hispanics or LatinXs. Africans have become known as African Americans. Today, together, they comprise upwards of 35% of the population of the country. White supremacy groups and conservative political groups have therefore targeted these two groups for voter suppression and disenfranchisement.

<u>1619</u>

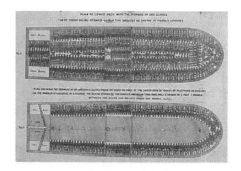

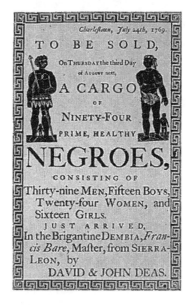

For 189 years (1619-1808) the British and the United States of America profited from the transatlantic slave trade. The end of the transatlantic slave trade did not mean the end of slavery. The United States ended their role in the transatlantic slave trade reluctantly. First of all, other European countries had already ended their participation in the business, and the U.S. had begun to increase their slave population exponentially through natural and forced reproductions. And of course, increases in slave population meant an increase in Congressional representation, which ultimately meant greater opportunities to maintain their system of human bondage.

The Impact of Race on The Whole of American Polity Throughout Her Historic Beginning

1846 – 1848

The Mexican – American War began in 1846 and lasted for two years. The war began because the U.S. wanted the territory of Texas and Mexico refused to sell. Due to the U.S.'s superior military might, the war was over in less than three years. Most politicians and citizens in northern states didn't necessarily want to go to war with Mexico over Texas. Texas had slaves, and if allowed in the Union as a slave state it would offset the balance of power between the northern and southern states that had been established with the Missouri Compromise of 1820. The acquisition of the State of Texas after the Mexican American War gave slaveholding states even more power. This was one of the causes of the Compromise of 1850 and later the Kansas – Nebraska Act of 1854. While these moves directly affected enslaved Africans, they also had a great impact on Mexican residents. The impact of the Mexican – American War on LatinXs in Texas and all over the southwest are still being felt today.

1860 - 1865

SECESSION AND THE CIVIL WAR

Statue of General George Gordon Meade at Gettysburg

"Val Atkinson Photos"

Ten of the eleven Confederate states refused to allow Abraham Lincoln's name on their ballot for President of the United States in the 1860 presidential general election. Led by South Carolina they seceded from the United States of America after Lincoln won the presidential election of 1860 to become the 16th President of the United States of America.

South Carolina officially seceded from the Union on December 20, 1860. Her secession was followed by six other southern states (Mississippi, Louisiana, Texas, Alabama, Florida and Georgia). At the time of secession, South Carolina and Mississippi had African slave populations that were greater than their white populations. The fear that drove most southern states to join the Confederacy was that the newly formed Republican Party and its chosen leader President Abraham Lincoln would soon end slavery and thereby their way of life.

Subsequently, after the war, many former Confederates blamed African Americans for their misfortunes. This sentiment started the "Tit for Tat" paradigm that remains with us today. All this led up to conscience efforts to disenfranchise African Americans.

1865 – 1877

RECONSTRUCTION

Reconstruction was an outgrowth of the Freedmen's Bureau Act, which was established to protect the rights of the formally enslaved and newly freed Africans. The 13th, 14th, and 15th Amendments are referred to as *"The Reconstruction Amendments"*. The 13th Abolished slavery, the 14th gave the former enslaved people citizenship, and the 15th gave the formally enslaved men the right to vote.

In the election of 1876 Sam Tilden and Rutherford B. Hayes compromised to bring a close to a very close and contentious race which allowed Hayes to become president and in return Hayes would not run for reelection and would remove the remaining troops from the south that were there to enforce to provisions of the Freedmen's Bureau Act. This effectively ended Reconstruction and gave the Confederacy their cultural victory.

After the assassination of Abraham Lincoln, Andrew Johnson became the 17th President of the United States of America. President Johnson was not a friend of the newly freed African Americans. Technically, he ended-up returning the land owned by African Americans to their slave masters and required African Americans to sign labor contracts with their former slave owners or face incarceration for vagrancy.

1877 - Present

POST RECONSTRUCTION

Black Codes, Jim Crow, The War On Drugs, Mass Incarceration, "Tit for Tat"

Before this discussion begins there must be a discussion about a reason for the Civil War not usually discussed. The usual culprits for the causes of the Civil War range from Sectionalism to Territories, to States' Rights, to Slavery; but rarely is white supremacy discussed as a reason for the Civil War. There is evidence that white supremacy is the common thread that connects all the rest, from Black Codes and Jim Crow to the War on Drugs and its resulting Mass Incarceration. When we examine these reasons through the lens of *"Tit for Tat"*, it becomes clear that race and white supremacy played **_The_** major role in the Civil War.

There is a school of thought that believes the south actually won the Civil War. The thought is based on the reasoning that the Union may have won the military and political war, but the south won the social and cultural war [*or white supremacy*]. The north did not fight the Civil War over racial supremacy as much as they fought over reunification. So, if the south came back into the union and accepted the 13th Amendment, there were those in the north that weren't really disturbed when black rights were being violated and whites were still exhibiting antebellum social and cultural behavior towards blacks. And this antebellum social and cultural behavior was all poor whites (soldiers who actually fought the war) wanted. So, after the assassination of President Lincoln, President Johnson literally restored the white supremacy culture the south had ostensibly lost after the Civil War. The Black Codes ensured the return to the *"Way of Life"* they have grown accustom to.

The Black Codes outraged public opinion in the North because it seemed the South was creating a form of quasi-slavery to negate the results of the war. When the Radical 39th Congress re-convened in December 1865, it was generally furious about the developments that had transpired during Johnson's Presidential Reconstruction. The Black Codes, along with the appointment of prominent Confederates to Congress, signified that the South had been emboldened by Johnson and intended to return to its old political order. This is when we began the Tit for Tat that continues to this very day.

"Tit for Tat" has permeated the American racial and socio-political continuum for as long as there has been a United States of America. We could rightly say it started with the Constitution itself. In Article II, Section 1 the Electoral College is established. This was an olive branch thrown at the slave holding states to get them to join the Union. After that it was the Missouri Compromise, and now runs through the election of Donald J. Trump.

TIT	**TAT**
Disagreements regarding where slavery will exist and will not exist	*The Missouri Compromise*
Fugitive Slave Act, and the Distribution of new territories taken from Mexico after the Mexican-American war	*The Compromise of 1850*
Non-slave states refusal to return run-a-way formerly enslaved persons	*The Compromise of 1850*
Lincoln is Elected as the nation's 16th president	*South Carolina Secedes from the Union in Dec. 1860*
Colonel Johnson refuses to surrender to General Beauregard	*The CSA fires on Fort Sumner "CIVIL WAR BEGINS"*
CSA remain in state of rebellion against the United States of America	*Emancipation Proclamation Issued*
CSA surrender to USA	*Reconstruction Amendments (13,14, & 15)*

13th Amendment Ratified 12/6/1865	*KKK founded in Pulaski, Tennessee 12/24/1865*
Freedman's Bureau gives land to formerly enslaved persons	*President Johnson returns land to defeated slaveholders*
Close contested election of 1876. Tilden compromises with Hayes	*Hayes ends Reconstruction by removing troops*
Former enslaved persons refuse to return to a state of slavery	*Mississippi Black Codes and the ensuing "Jim Crow Era"*
Democratic Party began to support desegregation (1948)	*Southern whites switched to the GOP*
The Supreme Court reversed "Plessey v Ferguson" in "Brown v. Board"	*The "White Citizens Council" was formed*
The 1964 Civil Rights Act was signed by President Johnson	*The "Southern Manifesto" was formed*
The 1965 Voting Rights Act was signed by President Johnson	*The "Southern Strategy" was formed by Harry Dent Sr.*
Social, economic and political advances made by African Americans	*The War on ~~Drugs~~ Black Men and Mass Incarceration*
Republicans win 5 of last 6 presidential elections ('68 – '88)	*Democrats establish DLC (Democratic Leadership Council) a Centrist Democratic Political Group*
Democrats win two election victories with Bill Clinton and Al Gore	*Electoral skullduggery (2000 Florida Vote Count)*
Two election victories by Barack Obama	*The Election of Donald J. Trump*
Hillary presents possibility of 16 years without a white male as president	*GOP get In bed with Russians to win the U.S. Presidency*
Voting demographics to change dramatically in 2045	*"Citizens United",*
Voting demographics changing too fast; and trending "WRONG"	*"Shelby v. Holder"*
State courts interfering with GOP Gerrymandering efforts	*"Rucho v. Common Cause*

Historians have described this system as the emergent result of a wide variety of laws and practices, conducted on all levels of jurisdiction. Because legal enforcement depended on so many different local codes, which underwent less scrutiny than statewide legislation, historians still lack a complete understanding of their full scope. It is clear, however, that even under military rule, local jurisdictions were able to continue a racist pattern of law enforcement, as long as it took place under a legal regime that was superficially race-neutral.

In 1893–1909 every Southern state except Tennessee passed new vagrancy laws. These laws were more severe than those passed in 1865, and used vague terms that granted wide powers to police officers enforcing the law. In wartime, Blacks might be disproportionately subjected to "work or fight" laws, which increased vagrancy penalties for those not in the military. The Supreme Court upheld racially discriminatory state laws and invalidated federal efforts to counteract them; in Plessy v. Ferguson (1896) it upheld the constitutionality of racial segregation and introduced the "separate but equal" doctrine.

A general system of legitimized anti-Black violence, as exemplified by the Ku Klux Klan, played a major role in enforcing the practical law of white supremacy. The constant threat of violence against Black people (and White people who sympathized with them) maintained a system of extralegal terror. Although this system is now well known for prohibiting Black suffrage after the Fifteenth Amendment, it also served to enforce coercive labor relations. Fear of random violence provided new support for a paternalistic relationship between plantation owners and their Black workers.

BLACK CODES

Mississippi:

Black Codes started in Mississippi. And because the codes were overtly racist many whites today don't think of themselves as racist because they can't imagine committing some the acts committed by white southerners against people of color. And yet the results are the same.

The codes were designed to return African Americans to a state of slavery ... As Doug Blackmon labeled it — *"Slavery by Another Name"*. The genius of the provisions in some of the codes were striking. They even had the nerve to euphemistically label one of their transgressions — *"An Act to confer Civil Rights on Freedmen"*. The provisions of the Act allowed blacks to rent land only within the city limits. This prevented blacks from making money as an independent farmer. Additionally the Act required blacks to present written proof that they were employed or they would face vagrancy charges.

South Carolina:

South Carolina's Black Codes allowed the state to hire-out blacks for no-pay.

Louisiana:

In Opelousas, Louisiana blacks had to have written authorization to enter the town.

Florida:

Florida's Black Codes made it possible for the children of blacks convicted of vagrancy could be hired-out as Apprentices. Additionally, black workers could be punished for disrespecting white employers.

North Carolina:

North Carolina established harsher sentences for blacks convicted of rape.

Texas:

Blacks were not allowed to vote, hold office, sit on juries, serve in local militia, carry guns, or attend public schools. Interracial marriage was also banned.

THE ELECTORAL COLLEGE's IMPACT ON
BLACK & BROWN VOTERS TODAY

Russian operative interfered with the United States presidential election of 2016. They did this by trying (and in some cases succeeding) at suppressing the black vote with disinformation campaigns.

African Americans are currently the 3rd largest racial/ethnic group in the country, behind Whites and Hispanics. As of 2019 there were 42 million African Americans living in the United States, comprising about 14 percent of the total. Fifty-five percent of African Americans live in the former Confederate states, and in 2016 *(because of the winner take all system of the Electoral College)* all of the former Confederate states *(save Virginia)* cast their votes for the candidate that received less than 10% of the African American vote, and the candidate that receive more than 90% of the votes representing more than 25 million people, receive absolutely zero votes from a total of 141 Electoral College votes cast from these 12 former Confederal states. As one African American voter from Raleigh, North Carolina put it … *"It's as though I voted for Donald J. Trump. I went to the polls to vote against him, but he ended-up with my support, my vote — he got all of North Carolina's votes regardless of who we voted for, and that's not fair".* It may not be fair but that the way the Electoral College system works. The good news is that there's something that can be done about it.

The representative share of the white population in the United States has been dropping over the last few decades. Whites are not reproducing at a rate high enough to offset the mortality rate, nor are they adding to the immigration number to out poll non-whites. These measures together spell a 'majority – minority' population in a few decades. GOP strategist have been aware of these numbers and the implications they portend for some time. Some have used these numbers in *"Dog Whistles"* to motivate whites to vote against their individual, personal self-interest, and vote for the continued domination of the white race by voting Republican. Some say it has worked, some ask at what cost. This *"Dog Whistle"* strategy is not a long-term strategy, but it's a very effective strategy to win an election here and there.

The Southern Strategy disallows any embrace of those considered to be the polar opposite of the old Confederacy. African Americans and Hispanics have not been loyal Grand Old Party supporters in past elections. With the exception of Cuban-Americans, the lion share of the Hispanic American vote generally goes to the Democratic candidate in presidential elections. Cuban Americans began their allegiance to the Republican Party after the failed *"Bay of Pigs"* incident. The Bay of Pigs was a failed attempt to overthrow the Fidel Castro regime and replace it with a pro-American government. Those Cubans that supported the American overthrow attempt were given a special *"Front of the Line"* pass when it came to Latino immigration to the U.S mainland. Cuban Americans therefore became loyal Republicans once that became citizens and received the right to vote. This was happening at a time before the 1965 Voting Rights Act was passed when African Americans were being systematically denied suffrage in any way imaginable. But after the Trump Administration's poor response to the damage caused by Hurricane Maria, and the attention given to building a wall on the southern border, many Latinos have left the Republican party, or at least halted their support of the Republican conservative causes.

Latinos and African Americans are the two largest non-white ethnic groups in the United States. Their combined total, along with other non-whites, will exceed 50% in 2046 or sooner. This is problematic for many Republicans, and just about all conservatives. Due to the strict ethnic positioning of those states that makeup the southern base of the Republican Party, their political tent will have a hard time expanding. If you tent is not expanding, and your mortality rate exceeds your procreation rate, establishing and maintaining a majority in the electorate will be difficult if not impossible.

Case in point: *In the last seven presidential elections the Republican candidate won the popular vote just ONCE! And yet, they secured the presidency in 3 of those 7 elections. This is all due to the Electoral College overriding the will of the American voter.*

These results have caused consternation in the African American community in particular, and as many have surmised, this serves as an internal voter suppression device. The Electoral College and everything that involves citizens' participation in the electoral process should stand for DEMOCRACY! Democracy doesn't just mean the absence of a tyrant, monarch, ruler, or king, it means that individual citizens actually decide (by their vote) who their leaders are going to be. Becoming the leader of the United States of America means leading all 326 million of the people, not just the people in Wisconsin, Michigan, Pennsylvania, North Carolina or Florida. It means being the leader of the people in Texas, Alabama, New York, and yes … even California. Voters shouldn't be discounted because they live in a prohibitively winnable or prohibitively losable state; nor should they have excessive value because they live in what has become known as a *"Battleground State"*.

If African American voters in New York and Georgia are experiencing similar problems they should be able to have their vote cast for the candidate they've determined to be their best bet to solve their problems. And definitely not have their votes cast for the candidate that has absolutely no regard for their issues. This is what the Electoral College as presently constructed allows. On November 8, 2016, the majority of African American voters in Mississippi went to the polls and voted over-whelmingly (90%+) for Hillary Clinton. Thirty-eight percent of the population in Mississippi is African American, and yet, Hillary Clinton's opponent in the 2016 presidential election (Donald J. Trump) garnered *"ALL"* of Mississippi's 6 electoral votes. What happened to the votes for Hillary Clinton cast by African Americans? They all went to Donald J. Trump — each and every one! This is called the Unit or WTA (winner take all) system in the Electoral College — *"not good for black and brown voters"*.

By 2050, the US will be a 'majority-minority' country, with white non-Hispanics making up less than half of the total population. The non-Hispanic white population is not growing as quickly as other groups in the U.S. Since the settlement of Jamestown in 1607 and the start of the Colonial period, the U.S. has been predominantly white. But the white share of the U.S. population has been dropping, from a little under 90% in 1950 to 60% in 2018. It will likely drop below 50% in another 25 years.

This is where it all comes to rest — *"the Electoral College"*. We began with the Reconstruction Amendments (13th, 14th, 15th, Amendments) and then it was the 19th, 23rd, 24th, and 26th, Amendments, so the next logical step is to do something about the Electoral College to make all the other attempts at equality and one person, one vote really mean something. We struggle through the 1965 Voting Rights Act and all the various 25 year renewals, only to come to Shelby Co. *v* Holder where it was miraculously learned that Section 4 of the 1965 Voting Rights Act was unconstitutional.

The plaintiffs charged that Section 4 of the act was unconstitutional because it cited circumstances that were over 50 years old as the reason they were under the auspices of the Act. *Section 4 states that if in 1964 your state or region of the state had less than 50% of its voting age population registered to vote, or less than 50% of those registered actually voted, the state of region became under the auspices of the 1965 Voting Rights Act.* Shelby augured that they should not be measured by 1964 standards, but by current standards, and there was no provision under current law for the sin of 1964 to be forgiven. The Supreme Court agreed with the plaintiff and struck-down Section 4 of the Act, directing the Congress to re-write that portion of the law. Of course, in the mean-time, there were no conditions to measure whether a state or region thereof came under the auspices of the 1965 Voting Rights Act. The Act became moot. Immediate after the court's ruling, the legislatures of Texas, Pennsylvania and North Carolina passed draconian voter suppression laws knowing that the 1965 Voting Rights Act had been effectively *"defanged"* and there was no longer any head-winds against moving back to pre-1965 voting conditions in all states.

REMEDIES:

Twenty-Eighth Amendment, Feasible Replacements for the current
System (Direct Elections, NPVIC, Proportional Distribution, Bonus System)
Positive Political changes emanating from the elimination of the Electoral College
(Federalizing Presidential Elections would: Facilitate Universal Suffrage, Eliminate
State Initiated Voter Suppression, and Improper Voter File Purging)

DISTRICT VOTE:

The *District Vote* is an alternative to the current application of the Electoral College, in that it would eliminate the WTA (winner take all) method of distributing the vote of the electors. Under the District Vote option, states would award candidates Electoral College votes based on the number of congressional districts in which they won the popular vote. The candidate receiving the most votes statewide would be awarded 2 additional votes to account for the 2 U.S. Senators representing the state. The District Vote differs from Proportional Allocation in that there would be no fractional votes to consider. The advantage of this system over the present system is that it wouldn't take the votes in NC Congressional Districts 1, 4, and 12 (that happened to vote for Hillary Clinton in 2016) and give those votes to her opponent — Donald J. Trump. In North Carolina Trump collected 2,362,631 votes to Clinton's 2,189,316 (a difference of 173,315 votes with a winning percentage of 49.83% to 46.17%). If Clinton received 46.17 percent of the vote shouldn't she have received 7 Electoral College votes? Why take her 7 votes and *"Give"* them to Donald Trump? This is not just a North Carolina problem — it happened all over America except Maine and Nebraska.

PROPORTIONAL ALLOCATION:

The *Proportional Allocation* alternative is presently being practiced by two states (Maine since 1972, and Nebraska since 1992). Proportional Allocations would also eliminate the *Unit Rule* which we presently operate under and replace it with a system that allows votes to have a more direct say in who their elected leaders will be. Under this alternative candidates would receive a proportion of the Electoral College votes commensurate with the proportion of the popular vote they garnered. This brings into play the possibility of candidates being authorized fractions of electors, i.e., 7.5% or 7.65%. And while electors cannot be dissected into fractions the fractions can be rounded to effectuate a whole number. Here again the alternative eliminates the possibility of candidates votes being taken and given to candidates they were not intended for. And the winner in this system will always be the candidate for whom the greatest number of votes were cast.

NATIONAL BONUS PLAN:

In this plan each candidate would win one Electoral College vote for each Congressional District he/she wins. This of course would leave each state 2 votes short of their total. To compensate for this shortfall there will be a bonus of 102 Electoral College votes awarded to the winner of the popular vote — guaranteeing that the popular vote winner wins the presidency. The new total votes needed to become president would be 321 of 640 Electoral College votes.

ABOLISH THE ELECTORAL COLLEGE:

First of all, the abolishment of the Electoral College would require a constitutional amendment. The founders wanted to ensured that it would not be easy to change the constitution so they involved both houses of congress and the individual states. The amendment process requires 2/3 approval in both houses (290 of 435 votes in the House and 67 of 100 votes in the Senate and ratification by — of the states, 38 of the 50 states).

NPVIC: *(National Popular Vote Interstate Compact)*

The *National Popular Vote Interstate Compact* is already underway. As of this writing there are 196 Electoral College votes committed by 16 states that amount to 73% of the of Electoral College votes needed to ensure that the winner of the popular vote also wins the Electoral College vote. Interestingly enough, of the old Confederate states, none have committed to the National Popular Vote Interstate Compact. There are three old Confederate states that have bills pending in State Legislative Committees (South Carolina, Georgia and North Carolina). Two states have yet to introduce NPVIC legislation (Texas and Tennessee). The remaining old Confederate states (Virginia, Alabama, Florida, Mississippi, Louisiana and Arkansas) have voted *"No"* to an NPVIC in their state.

We could go further and run cross tabs on the states that voted for Trump in 2020, or states that ranked very high in conservative polling, and we'd find the same results. Conservatives, supporters of the old Confederacy, and Republicans all want to retain the Electoral College and are therefore against any measure that would replace the best electoral tool they have for *"snatching victory from the jaws of defeat by the people's vote"*. But all that aside, the NPVIC is a viable replacement for the way we presently run the Electoral College. This method is preferred by many because it doesn't require a constitutional amendment. The drawback to the NPVIC is that it can be overturned with the up or down vote of state legislatures. But still, it would be more in the hands of the people than the current system is.

Unfortunately, the Electoral College is one of the most effective tools the ***"Right"*** uses to suppress the vote of minorities. When all else fails (voter intimidation, disinformation, precinct manipulation, voter file purge, disallowing early voting and extended operational hours, requiring voter I.D., and racial gerrymandering) the backstop for the ***"Right"*** has always been the **Electoral College**.

Minorities in states like Mississippi and Texas have to first out-vote the majority white voters, battle voter suppression, and then just maybe they'll have a chance to have their votes delivered to the candidate they intended to vote for all along. The citizens of the greatest democracy in the world deserve a better system than the Electoral College.

The "Concluding Rabbit" — Hidden in Plain Sight

"Val Atkinson Photos"

CONCLUSION

One cannot accurately assess the Electoral College, American politics, or the *American Experiment* without first considering America's attempt at establishing its own version of Western Civilization.

Since 1492 white men in America have been busy creating a *"new culture"* for European white males. That culture is based on the European descending hierarchy of royalty to serfdom. In the *old country*, it was easy to determine who was whom because everything was based on *blood-lines*. You had the royal DNA or you didn't. And it really **did** matter who your father was.

So it seems that the paradigm of Royalty to Serfdom might not be a bad idea if we could figure-out how to make everyone descendants of Royalty *(but you can't have mountains without valleys)*. Then someone figured-out that Serfs could be made to feel comfortable with their status if they just had someone they could look down upon. Then came the settlement of the so called *"New World"* and the genocide of the Native American population. White people found themselves hating Native Americans for reasons they couldn't quite explain; they just knew they hated them. And along with that hatred came the acceptance of displacement, murder and ultimately, genocide. And while this was happening there was lots and lots of money being made. A great deal of this new money was being made in southern states where the soil was perfect for raising tobacco, cotton and sugar cane. They found that Native Americans would not submit to chattel slavery, but there was a group discovered by the Portuguese in 1441 that would turn-out to be exactly what Europeans needed in the *"New World"* — **Enslaved People From Africa!**

Colonist joined the Transatlantic Slave Trade in 1619 and stayed in it for 189 years; and another 57 years of legal slavery after that. Doug Blackmon, in his book *"Slavery by Another Name"*, cites innumerable accounts of the continuation of an illegal, inhumane system for another

100 years after it was legally abolished in 1865. The reason it had such a long shelve life was the riches it produced and the cultural binding it manifested in the pursuit of a new brand of Western Civilization.

Africans were the perfect foil for this new European experiment. They looked different, they didn't speak any European language, they appeared to be docile and domestically manageable, and their historical and geographical orientations had been stripped from them. They could therefore be fed any foundational information the Europeans decided to feed them. This worked well for the enslavers. They forbade Africans to read, and anyone caught teaching Africans to read was severely punished. Some Africans began to accept their slave master's view of themselves (lazy, unintelligent, non-trustworthy, and dependent). Many fought against this faux indoctrination and started a movement that's still with us today — *The Civil Rights Movement.*

America's Electoral College problem is not a problem that affects the U.S. only. The whole world is watching ... especially those countries that we were, or are, involved in their *Nation Building.* They're looking to us for leadership, they look at us as a model of what they want to become. It's also interesting that of all the nation states around the world that we've influenced or mandated their polity, none have an Electoral College System. Maybe there's a reason for that.

Through it all I've concluded that the title of George C. Edwards III book **"Why the Electoral College is Bad for America"** has been answered. The reason is that it's bad for black and brown people, and therefore it's not good for all Americans. And when you have a political system that discriminates against a sizable portion of your people, it's not a just system and most importantly, it cannot be accurately be called a Democracy.

The Electoral College system needs to be replaced. Whether we replace it with the passage of an amendment to our constitution or institute one of the remedies (Proportional Distribution, District System with the two senatorial votes going to the winner of the popular vote, The Bonus System, or the NPVIC) we must move to save our Democracy by replacing this outdated archaic system.

I'm not sure that we need a Constitutional Convention to resolve this and other problems; but if a Constitutional Convention were to be called, I would support it wholeheartedly. The Electoral College has out-lived its usefulness and it has been coopted by a minority party that has used the Electoral College's short comings to win elections they could not win in a fair democratic election. The unconditional surrender of the Confederate States of America, the ratification of the 13th, 14th, and 15th Amendments, the onset of radio, and television, the passage of the 1964 CRA and the 1965 VRA, the advent of the internet and the resulting *social media* have all made the Electoral College ***totally unnecessary***!

The only purpose the Electoral College presently serves is to allow small states and former slaveholding states to have a greater say in how present-day America is to be run. This is when the re-reading of Article I of the Constitution should be mandatory for all those who still support the Electoral College for the sake of the small and former slaveholding states.

First of all, the Connecticut plan gave small states as much power as larger states when it established the U.S. Senate as one of the bicameral houses of the national legislature. And in the antebellum south, the slaveholding states enjoyed over-representation in the House of Representatives due to the 3/5 compromise. And then they were given a 20% bump when the 14th Amendment were ratified. So, the abolition of slavery actually gave the slaveholding states more congressional representation than they had during slavery. But their problem came when they decided that they didn't want to abide by the 15th Amendment — they wanted to **count** the former enslaved citizen, but they didn't want them to participate in the electoral process. Some still feel that way today, and they're using the Electoral College to help them win elections they should not win.

For once and for all, we need to stop letting Iowa and New Hampshire set the tone for our presidential elections, and we need to stop letting Florida, North Carolina, and Pennsylvania be the perennial states that decide for the rest of us who the next President of the United States of America will be. These three states comprise about 13% of the nation's population, and yet they are the battleground states that determine who will govern themselves and the other 87% of the population.

Presidential candidates tend to fashion their campaign rhetoric to satisfy (almost exclusively) the citizens of these battleground states. What about the other 87% of Americans? Don't they matter? We need a system that does what Jesse Wegman begs in his new book — **"Let the People Pick the President"**. If we had a presidential electoral system based on *popular plurality*, every vote would carry the same weight regardless of where it is cast. All states would be battleground states because all people would hear the same message. And candidates couldn't decide against visiting California, New York, Ohio, or Texas because they're prohibitably winnable or prohibitably losable states. Every time a candidate picks up a microphone he should be talking to all the people in America, not just the ones in the battleground states. The elimination of the Electoral College would make it so!

After the Electoral College is exorcised, the African American vote and the Hispanic vote will be heard. This means a political platonic shift in the way the two-party system has functioned electorally since its inception. Republicans will no longer be able to claim the solid south as their own, and Democrats will have to stop assuming that the south is unwinnable. The elimination of the Electoral College could change the title of Carol Anderson's book from "One Person No Vote" to "One Person One Vote". Once the people get to elect the president and vice president with their unfettered votes, and once one vote in New York counts just as much as one vote in North Carolina, then true democracy will flow like mighty rivers returning to the sea.

AFTERWORD

"CONNECTIONS"

Val Atkinson & Ed Clark — Host & Co-Host

Courtesy, Val Atkinson Photos

*"This photo says it **all** about competition, rivalry, and respect — neither of which were associated with the relationship between Democrats and Republicans in the presidential election of 2020".*

I n this section I will examine relevant issues that surfaced after the completion of the book but before publication. There were several categories of interest, not the least of which were the Supreme Court rulings on the LGBTQ Employment ruling the DACA decision, and of course, the unanimous ruling on the *"Faithless Electors"* case. The other impactful occurrences were the George Floyd and Breanna Taylor murders, the Covid -19 Pandemic, and of course the Biden & Harris presidential victory.

The Covid-19 virus may have begun in Wuhan, China, but it had its greatest impact in the United States of America. And why was this? One reason was the nature of America's socio-economic footprint. The culture practiced by most middle and upper class Americans, *and comparatively by all white Americans,* seeks maximum personal liberty and social choice. These are cultural elements that don't sit very well with the edict of *"ware your mask, wash your hands, and practice social distancing".* The engine of the American economy is *"Consumerism"* and the I.D. of its culture is *"Freedom, Liberty, and Individuality".* Americans are gregarious, ostentatious and generally fun loving. To inhibit their freedom of choice, predetermine their schedules and associates is an anathema to all that is Americana. It has not been surprising to this author that Americans makeup 4.6% of the world's population but over 20% of the positive cases of Covid – 19. Americans are a free spirited people, even in the face of death itself. These social practices don't bode well with best practices for controlling the spread of Covid-19. Additionally, some conservative Trump supporters saw the virus as something that liberals applauded to halt the economy and hamper the reelection chances of Donald Trump. They therefore refused to wear mask or practice social distancing to show their disbelief of the virus warnings being spread by *liberals* — who had control over the scientist.

Many GOP controlled state legislatures and governors fought against increased *"Mail-in"* voting to counter the effects of the spread of Covid-19. This was meant to have a negative impact in black and brown communities where wage workers can't afford to take off work, and stand in long lines (without social distancing) to cast their ballots. How did we get so polarized that a deadly pandemic with the capability to destroy our nation has become politized? We seem to be polarized on issues of war and peace, the economy, and all things racial, ethnic and social. Is there anything left that will unify Americans again?

The George Floyd murder was different but coincided with Covid-19, in that many of those who followed the stay-at-home recommendations and mandates by their state and local elected officials had become victims of cabin fever themselves and welcomed the opportunity to hit the streets and protest the murder of another unarmed black man at the hands of a white police officer. The protest took-on the name *"Black Lives Matter"*, even though in many protests a very large percentage of the protester were white. Across all sectors of society, reaching every crevasse and ravine the once besmudged Black Lives Matter movement became a rallying cry around which thousands gathered to chant the slogan *"Black Lives Matter"* and *"Enough is Enough"*. The interesting thing about the Black Lives Matter movement was that it occurred in all 50 states, the District of Columbia and overseas on six continents and in more than 24 countries, among them were: Brazil, Belgium, Netherlands, UK, Spain, Kenya, Portugal, South Korea, Australia, Syria, France, Sweden, South Africa, Denmark, Japan, Canada, Mexico, Germany and others. What this means is that the world is trying to tell the United States that they're not happy with the way she treats her citizens based on their race. They don't condone racism, and are beginning to question whether the United States of America is in any position to lecture the rest of the world about *"Human Rights Abuses"*.

One of the decisions released by the Supreme Court in June of 2019 is going to allow partisan state legislatures to Gerrymander their congressional and state legislative districts as they see fit. The court might as well have given states the authority to suspend future state legislature elections, thereby guaranteeing the Republican domination of some state legislatures indefinitely.

This decision is what Tom Hamburger and Peter Wallsten had in mind when they wrote the book *"One Party Country"*. This decision gives those states with a clear majority in either party an opportunity to keep that majority indefinitely. For the GOP, this is a great opportunity to close the lid on state politics in the United States of America, permanently. At the time of this book's publication the GOP controlled more state legislatures than ever before in its party's history. Presently the GOP holds both chambers in 32 states. They hold the upper chamber alone in 34 states and the lower chamber alone in 31 states.

This pro-Gerrymandering decision was the final coat of shellac on the *Shelby Co. v. Holder* decision that effectively gutted the 1965 Voting Rights Act. What the Rucho *v.* Common Cause decision allows is for the reining political party to write its own rules, choose its own voters, but more importantly, draft and pass the laws that govern what they can and can't do regarding the electoral process. This change in American politics could be the making of a permanent *"One Party Country"* for us all.

After the 1965 Voting Rights Act was enacted, Republicans knew they couldn't win very many heads-up fair elections against the Democrats. They also knew that it would be a losing trade-off to exchange the suburban and rural white voters for new black and brown voters; so, the obvious answer was *"voter suppression"*. Shelby Co. *v.* Holder set the stage for voter suppression in that they no longer had to get their voting procedure changes precleared before implementation. If Republicans don't take back the House of Representatives in 2022 it's because *"they ain't tryin'"*. They'll be free to redraw congressional district lines as they see fit. And with the sophisticated software used to Gerrymander, it should be a breeze. Additionally, every state legislature they recapture from Democrats is another state that will Gerrymander its own districts without oversight from the Justice Department or the Courts. On the other hand, if Democrats retain the House, retake the Presidency and the U.S. Senate, will they have the courage to renovate the draconian measures installed by the McConnell senate? That's the 64 thousand dollar question!

The Supreme Court Ruling on "Faithless Electors" may not have the impact that some think it will. The court ruled unanimously that Faithless Electors must follow the guidelines and rules of the state they represent. Each State will retain the authority to determine how and for whom their electors will cast their votes. Before this court ruling each state and the District of Columbia had rules regarding how electors would cast votes and types and durations of penalties for non-compliance with the state's electors' voting rules. This case was about whether electors would be allowed to become *"Free Agents"* and vote their conscience without regards to the wishes of the voters they ostensibly represent. The court's ruling confirmed what was already a practice of the Electoral College. There have been no elections where rouge electors decided the outcome of an election and there has always been faithless electors. In the 2016 presidential election there were seven faithless electors. They hailed from the states of Hawaii, Texas, and Washington. In Hawaii David Mulinix voted for Bernie Sanders instead of Hillary Clinton, in Texas Christopher Suprun voted for John Kasich instead of Donald Trump, and Bill Greene voted for Ron Paul instead of Donald Trump. In the state of Washington Levi Guerra, Esther John and Bret Chiafalo all voted for General Colin Powell instead of Hillary Clinton, and Robert Satiacum Jr. voted for Faith Spotted Eagle instead of Hillary Clinton. If all seven of these electors would have voted as pledged Trump would have totaled 306 electoral college votes while Clinton would have totaled 232. More importantly, this court decision has no effect on the NPVIC. States will still be able to advise their electors to cast their votes for the winner of the national popular vote — thereby ensuring that the people's choice for president doesn't lose the election because of an archaic 18th century electoral system call the Electoral College.

CENSUS

Another piece of the political puzzle of 2020 was the Decennial Census. This systematic enumeration of all persons living in the United States happens every ten years. It is a count of *All Persons*, not just all citizens. The results of the Census are used to determine the allocation of federal resources and to make future logistical plans. But the primary purpose of the Decennial Census is to determine the proportionality of representation in the U.S. House of Representatives. In 1929 the Congress determined that the number of voting U.S. Representatives would be 435. This is the base number for determining the number of Congressional Districts each state would be authorized. The formula is: *The total U.S. population divided by 435 = 1 Congressional District, i.e., 325,000,000 / 435 = 747,126.* This means that states will be apportioned 1 Congressional District for every group of 747,126 people that reside in their state, but no state will have less than 1 Congressional District. The 23rd Amendment to the United States Constitution considers the District of Columbia to be a state for the purposes of Electoral College voting. This raises the total number of Electoral College votes to 436 from the House and 102 from the Senate for a total of 538 Electoral College. If two candidates evenly split the total Electoral College votes, each candidate would have 269 votes. Therefore the required number for winning is 270 Electoral College votes. So, the Decennial Census has a direct impact on the Electoral College and for whom we cast our votes.

ELECTORAL COLLEGE

Unscrupulous political players could greatly impair our electoral process by defrauding the Decennial Census. The accurate and complete collection of data for the Decennial Census is therefore a crucial piece of the electoral process if a fair election is to be held.

And finally — probably the most compelling reason for changing or eliminating the Electoral College occurred immediately after the 2020 presidential election. The results clearly showed that Joe Biden had won the 2020 presidential election by over 6 million votes; and yet Donald John Trump refused to admit defeat. This is *after* Biden had been declared the winner by all the broadcast networks. Since the 1948 election, the TV networks have declared the winner of the election based on who won the popular vote of the various states and the total number of electoral college votes the states had. Traditionally, the runner-up in the presidential election would call the declared winner, congratulate him and concede the race. This didn't happen in the 2020 election for president. Instead, DJT proceeded to launch a tirade of lawsuits and other legal proceeding to reverse the election. Based on the popular vote tallies of the various states, the final electoral college vote total will be: Biden as 306, Trump 232. Candidates need 270 electoral college votes to win.

This was the first time in modern history that the losing candidate refused to concede the election in the face of overwhelming evidence. This may be the final nail in the coffin of the Electoral College. Politicians of goodwill on both sides of the aisle will get together and hammer-out some remedies for what has been a truly disastrous attempt to peacefully transfer power. Without some meaningful attempt to prevent this from happening again, we're all just standing with our hands behind our back (*fingers crossed*) hoping things will be different next time. Finger-crossed, hoping is not the best strategy for the times we find ourselves in.

Photo taken by "Val Atkinson Photos" for The Electoral College and the Black & Brown Vote"

"January 20, 2021"

And so it finally came to be — "The Election of the Century is Finally Over".

The general election of 2020 will go down in American history as one of the most directional election in the nation's history. One-hundred and fifty-six years after the directional election of 1864 we witnessed the other mega-directional election. The election of 1864 was held in the midst of the Civil War, and everyone knew that the outcome could have determined who won the war. General George B. McClelland, the Democratic candidate that ran against the incumbent Republican (Abraham Lincoln) ran on his commitment to end the Civil War by allowing the Confederacy to have their own nation. Lincoln, of course, wanted to preserve the nation and fought to defeat the Confederacy.

In the election of 2020 the choice was also clear: Joe Biden, who served 6 terms (36 years) as Delaware's senior U. S. Senator, and two-terms (8-years) as the U.S. Vice President under President Barack Obama from 2009 until 2017: or Donald J. Trump who never served in the military or public life, and has made a living on the inheritance left to him by his grandfather, Fred Trump. Donald Trump was a *Reality TV Host and Real Estate Entrepreneur*. He dodged the draft by claiming he had bone spurs in one of his legs. He had two failed marriages, five bankruptcies and is in debt to unknown debtors for over $400,000,000.00. There were over two dozen women that charge him with sexual harassment and/or sexual assault. He paid a prostitute to **NOT** file charges against him before the election, and he was recorded on tape as saying *"You can grab beautiful women by the Pussy and they won't say anything if you're famous"*. This is the guy you don't want you son to emulate when he grows-up, and you cover your daughter's ears when he's talking — and yet you want him to be the president of the United States of America, **WHY? Pray Tell WHY?**

In 2016 Trump received 62,984,828 popular votes, while Hillary received almost 3 million more (65,853,514). But because the Electoral College awards the election to the candidate that receives 270 or more Electoral College votes, Hillary Clinton became the 5th candidate in U.S. presidential history that got more popular votes than her opponent, but did not win the presidency.

On November 3, 2020, I sat in my mancave watching the returns on MSNBC, CNN and FOX News. I knew that there was a chance that all the battleground states' results wouldn't be in by election night, so I was prepared to **wait**. And wait I did. It wasn't until November 8, 2020 that the networks announced the perceived President Elect — *"The Honorable Joe Biden"*! Then we played the waiting game. Donald Trump was supposed to utter the words … *"I LOST"*. But did he? If he would have, would his entire suit of fabricated armor fall completely apart? Instead of conceding, he took the country through two and a half months of *"Political Hell"*. He refused to concede the election and start the all-important transition process. The transition process took-on added significance this time because of Covid-19. But that didn't matter to a self-indulged narcissist like Donald Trump. He always put himself first … even first before the country. I often wondered how could his supporters call themselves Americans while they allowed DJT to violate the law, put himself above the country and be the anti-role model for our children.

The subtitle of this piece is *"January 20, 2021"*. I chose that date because it's the date that the President Elect and Vice President Elect are sworn-in as the top chief executives of the United States of America. There were several pothole dates between November 3, 2020 and January 20, 2021. The first was any date between November 3rd and December 8th. During this time the loser / losers could conceivably mount various challenges to the vote outcome {*and mount they did*}. This is a most dangerous time for American democracy. This needs to be fixed. During this time the various states go through various *vote certification* processes. At any step the losers could try to over-turn or refuse to certify a particular state's election. December 8th was Safe Harbor Date. This is when the electors got together in a preliminary fashion to ensure there were no problems that needed to be addressed before the election slated for December 14th. After the Electoral College votes on December 14th, the new congress is sworn-in on January 3, 2021, the Vice President reads the results before a joint session of Congress, on January 6, 2021 and the President Elect is sworn-in at noon on January 20, 2021.

Hallelujah, It's Over!!!

BIBLIOGRAPHY

Alexander, Michelle. *The New Jim Crow: Mass Incarceration in the Age of Colorblindness. New York, NY: New Press, 2010*

Alcoff, Linda. *The Future of Whiteness: Malden Mass: Polity Press, 2016*

Carol Anderson. *One Person, No Vote: New York, NY: Bloomsbury Publications, 2018*

Baptist, Edward. *The Half Has Never Been Told: New York, NY: Basic Books, 2014*

Berman, Ari. *Give Us The Ballot: New York, NY: FSG Press, 2020*

Bennett, Robert. *Taming The Electoral College: Stanford, California: Stanford University Press, 2006*

Del Blanco, Andrew. *The War Before The War: New York, NY: Penguin Press, 2014*

Di Angelo, Robin. *White Fragility: New York, NY: Beacon Press, 2018*

Drutman, Lee. *Breaking The Two-Party Doom Loop: New York, NY: Oxford University Press, 2020*

Edsall, Thomas. *Building Red America: New York, NY: Basic Books, 2006*

Edwards, George C. *Why The Electoral College Is Bad For America: New Haven, Connecticut: Yale University Press, 2004*

Fauntroy, Michael. *Republicans And The Black Vote: Boulder, Co: Rienner Publications, 2007*

Foner, Eric. *Reconstruction 1863-1877: New York, NY: Harper Books, 1988*

Fortier, John C. *After The People Vote: Washington, D.C.: AEI Press, 2004*

Lessig, Lawrence. *They Don't Represent Us: New York, NY: Harper Collins Publications, 2019*

Loomis and Shumaker. *Choosing A President: New York, NY: Chatham House Press, 2002*

McCarty, Nolan. *Polarized America: Cambridge, Massachusetts: MIT Press, 2006*

Pierson and Hacker. *Off Center: New Haven, Connecticut: Yale University Press, 2005*

Wallsten and Hamberger. *One Party Country: Hoboken, NJ: Wiley Publishing, 2006*

Wegman, Jesse. *Let The People Pick The President: New York, NY: St. Martin Press, 2020*

Made in the USA
Middletown, DE
28 March 2024

52203999R00085